Blessing
of the
Rosary

Also by Dennis J. Billy, C.Ss.R.

Experiencing God: Fostering a Contemplative Life

Plentiful Redemption:
An Introduction to Alphonsian Spirituality

Simple, Heartfelt Words:
Preaching in the Alphonsian Tradition

Soliloquy Prayer: Unfolding Our Hearts to God

There Is a Season: Living the Liturgical Year

The Way of a Pilgrim:
Complete Text and Reader's Guide

With Open Heart:
Spiritual Direction in the Alphonsian Tradition

Blessings
of the
Rosary

meditations
on the mysteries

DENNIS J. BILLY, C.SS.R.

Liguori
ONE LIGUORI DRIVE
LIGUORI MO 63057-9999

Imprimi Potest: Thomas D. Picton, C.Ss.R.
Provincial, Denver Province, The Redemptorists

Published by Liguori Publications, Liguori, Missouri
To order, call 800-325-9521 or visit www.liguori.org

Library of Congress Cataloging-in-Publication Data

Billy, Dennis Joseph.
    Blessings of the rosary : meditations on the mysteries / Dennis J. Billy. — 1st ed.
        p. cm.
    ISBN 978-0-7648-1943-8
    1. Mysteries of the Rosary. I. Title.
    BT303.B55 2010
    242'.74—dc22

                                                            2010009689

Liguori Publications, a nonprofit corporation, is an apostolate of the Redemptorists. To learn more about the Redemptorists, visit Redemptorists.com.

Printed in the United States of America
14 13 12 11 10   5 4 3 2 1
First Edition

In honor of
Mary, the Mother of God,
Our Mother of Perpetual Help

Christ is the supreme Teacher, the revealer and the one revealed. It is not just a question of learning what he taught but of "learning him". In this regard could we have any better teacher than Mary? From the divine standpoint, the Spirit is the interior teacher who leads us to the full truth of Christ (see Jn 14:26; 15:26; 16:13). But among creatures no one knows Christ better than Mary; no one can introduce us to a profound knowledge of his mystery better than his Mother.

POPE JOHN PAUL II
ROSARIUM VIRGINIS MARIAE, 14

CONTENTS

INTRODUCTION

On a recent visit to New York's Metropolitan Museum of Art, I was wandering through a display of medieval art when I came upon a wooden carving the size of a small grapefruit called *Rosary Bead*. The bead's exterior was intricately designed with a variety of Christian symbols, including crosses, candles, and doves. What surprised me about this piece, however, was not its exterior, but the way it opened to reveal in its interior—in even more finely crafted detail—a three-dimensional scene of Christ's crucifixion.

The artist had gone to great pains to recreate the scene of Jesus' death. Everything was there: Christ on the cross, the two thieves, Mary, the women and the beloved disciple at the foot of the cross, the soldiers, the crowd, the darkened sky—and all within a space the size of a grapefruit! Minute as they were, the details were so vivid that I could actually make out the crown of thorns on Jesus' head, the wounds in his hands and feet, and the blood pouring down the wound at his side.

I felt as though I was peering into another world. The mystery of Christ's passion and death had come to life within this small internal space. All I could do was stare into it and contemplate its meaning. I gradually saw that the craftsman was trying to reveal Christ's paschal mystery concealed within the bead itself—in this case, the crucifixion. We ourselves do much the same thing when we pray the rosary and reflect on its mysteries: We pray it so that its mysteries will come alive for us and help shape the way we view ourselves, others, and the world we live in.

The rosary is a simple prayer deeply rooted in the Catholic tradition. It can be prayed aloud or in silence, in private or in a group. Its purpose is to immerse us in the mysteries of the Christian faith through heartfelt prayers to Jesus and his mother, Mary.

Traditionally consisting of fifteen decades of one Our Father, ten Hail Marys, and one Glory Be to the Father, the rosary has often been called "the poor man's Psalter." These fifteen decades, which reflect the 150 Psalms of the Old Testament, were a means of giving the poor and illiterate a way to participate more deeply in mysteries of the faith.

The traditional fifteen decades are further arranged into five Joyful, five Sorrowful, and five Glorious Mysteries, which relate respectively to the Incarnation, Christ's passion and death, and the glories of Jesus and Mary. For those wishing to penetrate the Gospel message ever further, Pope John Paul II added five Luminous Mysteries (also called Mysteries of Light) relating to Jesus' public ministry. This addition expands the traditional arrangement to a full twenty decades.

In response to Pope John Paul II's 2002 call for theologians to help the Christian people "to discover the Biblical foundations, the spiritual riches and the pastoral value of this traditional prayer" (On the Most Holy Rosary [*Rosarium Virginis Mariae*], 43), this book offers a profound meditation on each Mystery of the twenty-decade rosary. My aim is to provide a prayerful reflection on each Mystery and then ask probing questions that will help readers deepen their awareness of God's action in their lives.

These meditations on the Mysteries of the Rosary are not only for newcomers to this venerable prayer form, but also for those who already practice it regularly and are interested in making it an even more integral part of their lives and daily devotion.

HOW TO USE THESE REFLECTIONS

Depending on the inclinations and needs of the reader, this book can be used for spiritual reading or in conjunction with the actual recitation of the rosary. It can be read in parts on the specific days allocated to each Mystery: the Joyful (Monday and Saturday), the Luminous (Thursday), the Sorrowful (Tuesday and Friday), and the Glorious (Wednesday and Sunday). It can also be read in conjunction with the liturgical seasons: the Joyful (Advent and Christmas), the Luminous (Ordinary Time), the Sorrowful (Lent) and the Glorious (Easter). Readers should use the book in whatever way they think will help them ponder more deeply the mysteries of this beautiful prayer in the recesses of their hearts. Such was Mary's way. By following it, we will be sure to walk in the footsteps of her Son.

"With the Rosary, the Christian people *sits at the school of Mary* and is led to contemplate the beauty on the face of Christ and to experience the depths of his love" (*RVM*, 1). These words of Pope John Paul II remind us why we pray the rosary. I hope these meditations on the twenty-decade rosary immerse readers in the waters of God's love and help them share it with others.

The school of Mary is first and foremost a school of Christian discipleship. As we finger the beads of her rosary, may the mysteries they represent open our minds to Christ's presence in our lives and, like Mary, help us respond to his call with every fiber of our being.

PART I

THE JOYFUL MYSTERIES

The first five Mysteries of the Rosary focus on the Incarnation, allowing us to ponder the joy of God's Word entering this world as a small child.

The first two decades look at events that took place prior to Jesus' birth: The *Annunciation* contemplates the Angel Gabriel's message to Mary that she would conceive by the Holy Spirit and bear a son. The *Visitation* looks at Mary's visit to her kinswoman, Elizabeth, who in her old age has conceived a son who will prepare the way for the Messiah. These mysteries remind us that nothing is impossible for God. They show us how God has prepared for his entrance into the world by mysterious means: a virgin birth and the arrival on the scene of a great prophetic figure.

The third decade, the *Nativity of Our Lord,* contemplates the central event of the Incarnation. It ponders both the poverty into which Jesus was born and the great miracle of love his birth represents. This Mystery reminds us that God first experienced our world through the weakness and frailty of an infant and invites us to get in touch with those same qualities in our own lives.

The final two decades look at events after Jesus' birth. The *Presentation in the Temple* looks at the joy surrounding Jesus' consecration to God and the prophetic utterances accompanying it. The *Finding in the Temple* shows us how, even at a very young age, Jesus was growing in wisdom and involved in his Father's affairs. These mysteries remind us of Jesus' early life blessed by God in every way. They help us contemplate the mystery of the Word of God, who not only entered our world, but also grew in age and wisdom under the watchful gaze of his parents.

Taken together, the first five Mysteries of the Rosary concentrate on events that took place before, during, and after Jesus' entrance into the world. They remind us of the great joy surrounding his birth and childhood.

We meditate upon these Mysteries of the Rosary to share in that joy.

FIRST JOYFUL MYSTERY

THE ANNUNCIATION

Rejoice, O highly favored daughter!
The Lord is with you.
LUKE 1:28

The first Joyful Mystery depicts Mary's encounter with Gabriel, one of the four archangels of the Hebrew tradition. In Hebrew, *Gabriel* means "God is a strong man" or "strong man of God." The message the angel bears speaks of God's power and might. With God, all things are possible. He can even enter our world and become one of us.

We don't know exactly how Gabriel communicated God's message to Mary. Angels are immaterial creatures capable of communicating with human beings in a variety of ways.

The Gospel of Luke presents the encounter between Gabriel and the Virgin Mary as a simple dialogue. The angel comes to Mary and addresses her as God's highly favored daughter. Mary is at first troubled by his greeting but is told not to fear, for she has found favor with God. She will conceive and bear a son whom she is to name *Jesus*. He will be called "Son of the Most High" and shall ascend to the throne of David and rule over the house of Jacob forever.

Mary wonders how this can happen, since she is a virgin and has never been with a man. Gabriel responds that the Holy Spirit will come upon her and that the power of the Most High will overshadow her. She also receives a sign of the Lord's power and might. Elizabeth, her kinswoman, has conceived a son in her old age. Gabriel reminds Mary that nothing is impossible with God. At the end of the conversation, Mary responds with her humble and heart-warming *fiat*: "Behold, I am the handmaid of the Lord. May it be done to me according to your word" (Luke 1:38). Then the angel leaves.

Luke's account of the Annunciation does not pretend to be a detailed historical reconstruction of what took place. It's primarily a statement of faith in God's power to do the impossible and Mary's humble willingness to cooperate fully with the divine plan. Mary could have conversed with the angel as the scene describes, or a mental exchange of thought could have taken place. It's even possible that Mary became aware of the angel's message by means of a deep intuition, with no spoken words or silent thoughts.

However it happened, key elements of Luke's account ring true. Mary was troubled by what was being asked of her. She didn't understand how this promise could happen. She was being invited to trust in the power and love of God, and she did so with every fiber of her being.

The Annunciation scene culminates in Mary's humble *fiat*. Aware of the humiliation and rejection that might follow, she put herself at risk to participate in God's plan for humanity. Rather than look after her own interests, she trusted in the Lord's promise and opened both her heart and her womb to the gentle movement of the Spirit.

The Mystery of the Annunciation reminds us of God's invitation to all of us to join in his ongoing plan of redemption. Mary did so in a unique way by opening herself to the creative power of the Spirit in her life. Unlike Mary, we cannot give birth to the Word of God physically. She alone was specially prepared and chosen for that unique task. Never again in the history of humanity will someone again be called upon to do what she did. With Mary, however, we can give birth to God's Word within our hearts.

We do so by listening carefully to the words God gives us through the Scriptures, through creation, through the events of the day, through the people we meet, and through the still, small voice deep within our hearts.

Like Mary, we may be troubled by what we hear. Like Mary, we may not fully understand what God asks of us. Like Mary, we may feel ourselves to be inexperienced and wanting in knowledge.

One thing is certain: Like Mary, we are all called to trust in the Lord by placing our lives totally in his care. And we do so by allowing God to be God in our lives. Mary's *fiat* has initiated a process in which all of us are invited to take part. We too must respond to the Lord's messengers in our lives with the utter trust and total abandonment of the humble maiden of Galilee.

"Easier said than done," some of us may be thinking. And we would be right. Something more *is* required of us: We pray this joyful Mystery of the Rosary so that Mary's *fiat* might one day become fully ours. As we finger the beads one Hail Mary at a time and picture the scene of the Annunciation, we see that Mary's following of the Lord's command was not a single isolated action, but something repeated every day of her life. The repetition of our prayers reminds us of the many acts of love—both large and small—involved in the ongoing process of radical conversion. We pray to Mary because we need her help. We ask her to help us respond to God's will for us. We ask her to help us be generous with our hearts, ever ready and willing to serve wherever and whenever the need arises. We ask her to intercede for us, to pray for us so that we too might stand with her in the communion of saints.

There is only one Mystery of the Annunciation, but there are many annunciations in our lives. As we reflect upon this Joyful Mystery, let us ask the Lord for the grace to listen for the words he speaks to us, to ponder them in ours hearts and, like Mary, respond to them in love freely, fully, and faithfully every day of our lives.

Reflection Questions

- Have you ever sensed that God was asking something of you?
- If so, what was it?
- Did you ponder it?
- Were you troubled by it?
- How did you respond to it?
- Was your response similar to Mary's?
- How was it different?
- What effect did this invitation have on your life?
- Did it bring you closer to God or further away?
- Do you believe God's Word wishes to be born within your heart?
- Do you believe all things are possible with God?
- If not, why not? What can God not do?

SECOND JOYFUL MYSTERY

THE VISITATION

*And how does this happen to me,
that the mother of my Lord should come to me?*
LUKE 1:43

The second Joyful Mystery concerns Mary's visit to her kinswoman, Elizabeth who, according to the angel's message, had conceived a son in her old age. Even though she had just heard the startling news that she too would soon conceive and bear a son, Mary puts all thoughts of herself aside and immediately sets out from Galilee into the hill country to Elizabeth's house in a town of Judah.

This journey would have been rugged for anyone, let alone a pregnant woman journeying by foot. It meant covering a distance of at least thirty miles and would have taken Mary from Galilee through the neighboring region of Samaria and into Judea.

In this Mystery of the Rosary, we see why Mary is called "the handmaid of the Lord" (Luke 1:38). She who would soon give birth to Jesus, the man for others, reveals by her actions that she was truly a woman for others. She manifests her love for God through a life of humble service. Her meeting with Elizabeth exhibits her care for those in need and her willingness to go out of her way to help them.

The account of the Visitation appears only in Luke 1 and immediately follows the scene of the annunciation. As with the other infancy narratives, the details presented in this story are important not so much for their historical accuracy, but for the outlook of faith they support.

As we go through the scene, the particulars reveal to us the great depth of Mary's faith in the Lord. After hearing the angel's message, Mary sets out in haste to meet Elizabeth, traveling a great distance—from Galilee to Judah—to spend time with her kinswoman. When Elizabeth hears Mary's greeting, the baby leaps in her womb. Filled with the Holy Spirit, Elizabeth blesses the child in Mary's womb and wonders why the mother of her Lord would visit her. She shares with Mary the joy of the child stirring in her womb. Mary, in turn, responds with her Magnificat.

This great Christian hymn of joy rests at the very center of the visitation scene. Through it, we learn that Mary is not only faithful but also joyful in her service to others. Her actions flow from her very being and are rooted in her deeply loving and intimate relationship with her God.

Mary's prayer proclaims the greatness of God and all he does on behalf of the poor and the lowly. It's a declaration of God's faithfulness and of his ongoing presence in the lives of his people. Mary, we are told, stays with Elizabeth for about three months before returning home.

The account of the Visitation tells us that Mary is anxious to serve others, goes out of her way to do so, and does it with great joy. Because of her great trust in the Lord, she is able to let go of her own concerns, many as they are, and seek the well-being of others. Her trust in the Lord is the source of her great strength. As her Magnificat reveals, that strength stems from a rich and very deep life of prayer.

One cannot read the account of the Visitation without sensing that the words of the Magnificat have swelled up from deep within Mary and flow out her intimate communion with God. Mary is a woman of prayer because she is a woman of the Spirit.

God has chosen her and blessed her; she, in return, has blessed and chosen her Lord.

The Mystery of the Visitation isn't only about Mary's journey to her kinswoman Elizabeth. It's also our story. As we follow Mary through the hill country of Judah to meet her kinswoman, we see our own desire to put our own interests and concerns aside so that we can serve the needs of others. As the child leaps for joy in Elizabeth's womb when she hears Mary's greeting, we too are inwardly moved by the depth of Mary's love for God and her willingness to serve. As Elizabeth blesses the fruit of Mary's womb, we bless the Lord as he is being born within our hearts. As Mary's soul proclaims with joy the greatness of her Lord, we open our hearts to God in prayer and get in touch with our deep desire to be utterly one with him.

Throughout the account of the Visitation, Mary stands out as someone we not only admire, but also strive to be like. We journey with her; we serve with her; we pray with her. She is the disciple of Christ we earnestly desire to become.

And still there is something else. As we ponder the Mystery of the Visitation, we gradually come to see that Mary's visit to Elizabeth is only the beginning of a very important ministry. Mary visits each of us in our time of need. Her concern for us is probably even greater than her concern for her pregnant kinswoman. Elizabeth was bearing the precursor of Christ within her womb, but we are giving birth to the Divine Word within our hearts. His birth within us testifies to the power of God's mercy and transforming love.

Jesus entered our world not only to save us, but also to dwell within our hearts. Our ongoing conversion means that the Mystery of the Visitation must continue. Mary hastens to us. She goes out of her way to meet us. She greets us, comforts us, rejoices with us, and prays with us. She stays with us and beckons us to welcome her Son into her heart so that he can work his gentle magic in our hearts. She tells us of his power and might, but also of his mercy and faithfulness to those who fear him.

Mary desires only one thing: that her Magnificat might one day become fully our own so that *with her* we might proclaim with joy and without the slightest bit of hesitation the wonderful greatness of the Lord.

Reflection Questions

- Are there any people in your life whom God has called you to serve in a particular way?
- If so, who are they?
- How do you know them?
- What are their needs?
- Are you anxious to serve them?
- Do you go out of your way to do so?
- Do you do so with great joy?
- If not, what would make it easier for you to do so?
- What could you do or to whom could you turn?
- Do you find it difficult to put your needs aside for the sake of others?
- Have you ever asked God for help?
- Have you ever asked Mary?

THIRD JOYFUL MYSTERY

THE NATIVITY OF OUR LORD

*And this will be a sign for you: you will find an infant
wrapped in swaddling clothes and lying in a manger.*
LUKE 2:12

The third Joyful Mystery focuses on the birth of Jesus. The Gospels have two accounts of Jesus' birth. Matthew's version offers a genealogy of Jesus and stories about astrologers from the east following a star to Bethlehem, the Holy Family's flight into Egypt, the slaughter of the Holy Innocents, and the Holy Family's return to Nazareth (see chapters 1—2).

Luke's version follows his accounts of the Annunciation and Visitation. The birth takes place in a stable at Bethlehem in Judea, the city of David. With no room at the travelers' lodge, Jesus' parents placed him in a manger and wrapped him in swaddling clothes. The event was announced to nearby shepherds by an angel and a multitude of the heavenly host saying, "Glory to God in the highest and on earth peace to those on whom his favor rests" (2:1–20).

Although Matthew's and Luke's versions are distinct, most people blend them in their minds when they meditate on this Mystery of the Rosary.

Central to both stories, of course, is the birth of the child Jesus at Bethlehem. For Matthew, Jesus is *Emmanuel*, a name meaning, "God is with us" (1:23). For Luke, Jesus is the Savior of Israel, the Messiah and Lord (see 2:11). Both present the child Jesus as a manifestation of God's salvific promise. Jesus has come into the world for one reason only: to bring peace and salvation to the world.

For both, the Christmas story is all about God's powerful entrance into the world of human experience. Through Jesus, God is able to experience life through human senses. He can see, hear, taste, touch, and smell as we do. God entered our world, however, not merely to experience life through human eyes, but to heal us and raise us to new heights.

The Incarnation initiates a gradual and ongoing process of humanity's divinization that enables us to become what we are called by God to be. For a person to be fully alive, however, God must first dwell in his or her heart. The Word of God took on human flesh to manifest itself to us and live in our hearts. Because of Jesus' birth, we are given the opportunity to commune with God and to participate in the divine life in an intimate way.

The Christmas story celebrates this divine indwelling in the person of Jesus—and so very much more. It tells us of the goodness of creation, of God's love for humanity, and of humanity's deep hunger and inner longing for God. To say that God became man in Jesus is to assert the grandeur of God's love and its capacity both to heal and to radically transform the human heart.

Although God doesn't become human in us as he did in Jesus, the Christmas story reminds us of God's deep desire to enter our world, to give himself to us completely, to become nourishment and a source of hope for us. Because of Jesus' birth, the Word of God communes with us and is born within our hearts.

From the moment of Jesus' birth, new horizons have opened for humanity. Through Jesus, God revealed himself to us fully. The Mystery of the Nativity asks us to reciprocate by likewise opening our hearts to God.

"The Word became flesh and made his dwelling among us," (John 1:14). The Prologue of John's Gospel speaks of God's entrance into the world in a new and radically different way. By taking on human flesh, God has definitively entered human history; time and space now house divinity in a way never before thought possible. To assume this humanity, however, the Divine Word must drastically limit itself.

In his letter to the Philippians, the Apostle Paul speaks of a process of self-emptying that made the Incarnation possible: "Though he was in the form of God, [he]did not regard equality with God something to be grasped. Rather, he emptied himself, taking the form of a slave, coming in human likeness" (2:6–7).

God's purposeful self-containment makes the miracle of Christ's birth possible. Because of it, the divine poverty lies at the heart of every authentic human gift. The Astrologers recognized this when they laid their gifts of gold, frankincense, and myrrh beside the manger (see Matthew 2:11). We too understand this when we peer through the gifts we give and receive at Christmas and find the gentle presence of Christ in those we love.

The Christmas story emphasizes this process of self-emptying through Jesus' frailty and the situation of poverty into which he was born. His family had to make a difficult journey, crossing many miles from Galilee to Judea to Bethlehem. Once there, they could find no place to stay and were forced to take refuge in a cave or makeshift shelter. Jesus was born in the darkness and cold of night, wrapped in swaddling clothes, and laid in a manger, perhaps with a small fire and the breath of animals stabled there for night to keep him warm.

The poverty surrounding Jesus' entrance into the world reflects the way he emptied himself of divinity to become human. His outward poverty points to his deep inner poverty, which enabled him to humble himself before God and humanity.

The Mystery of the Nativity is all about God's journey to us and, ultimately, our journey to God. To enjoy an intimate relationship with the divine, we must take the Christmas story to heart. Like Jesus, we must empty ourselves so God can enter our hearts and dwell there. We must become like little children and recognize our inability to heal ourselves and make ourselves whole. We must embrace the poverty of our human situation and invite God to be a part of our lives.

The Christmas story rejoices in the presence of "Emmanuel, God with us." To celebrate it properly, we must look beyond the historical event of Christ's birth—important as it is—to the birth of the Divine Word within our hearts. For this reason, the celebration of Christmas is, of necessity, an ongoing story. It takes place whenever and wherever we make room for God in our hearts. The space we give him there needn't be grand. The wonder of Christmas is all about God showering his love upon the world and making do with little else.

Reflection Questions

- Is there room in your heart for God?
- What place have you prepared for him?
- Have you invited him in?
- Have you made him feel welcome and at home?
- Is Christmas an ongoing story in your life?
- Would you like it to be?
- If so, what could you do to make it so?
- What does it mean to allow God to be born in your heart?
- To dwell in your heart?
- To experience "paradise" in your heart?
- Have you ever given God the gift of your heart?
- Have you done so today?

FOURTH JOYFUL MYSTERY

THE PRESENTATION IN THE TEMPLE

They took him up to Jerusalem
to present him to the Lord.
LUKE 2:22

In the fourth Joyful Mystery, Jesus is brought to the temple and consecrated to God. He had already been circumcised and given his name (see Luke 2:21). According to the Book of Exodus, however, every firstborn son also had to be specifically presented and dedicated to the Lord (see Exodus 13:12). Mary and Joseph bring their son to the temple to fulfill this statute. Mary, his mother, also had to be purified through ritual sacrifice of "two turtledoves or two pigeons" (Leviticus 12:8). Luke goes to great lengths to show that Mary and Joseph have followed Hebrew Law assiduously. He seeks to present Jesus' parents as devout Jews who strictly observed all that was required of them by law, the implication being that Jesus would be steeped in the laws and traditions of his ancestors.

When Mary and Joseph bring in the child Jesus to carry out on his behalf the ritual required by law, they have a mysterious encounter with Simeon, a holy and pious man who, through the inspiration of the Holy Spirit, was told that he would not see death until he had seen the Messiah. As Mary and Joseph bring Jesus up to the temple, Simeon takes the child in his arms and blesses God in these words: "Now, Master, you may let your servant go in peace, according to your word, for my eyes have seen your salvation, which you prepared in sight of all the peoples, a light for revelation to the Gentiles, and glory for your people Israel" (Luke 2:29–32).

In his old age, Simeon stands at a transition point in history. He has been blessed with a glimpse of the passing from the Old Law to the New. Jesus, the Anointed One being presented to God in the temple, promises to transform the human heart itself into a temple of the Holy Spirit.

Simeon's testimony demonstrates that this redemptive work has already begun. His words have found their way into the Church's prayer and are now firmly rooted in the Christian imagination. Each night at the Liturgy of the Hours, Christians throughout the world are inspired by his words of inner longing and patient hope. As night descends upon the world, his words move us to look with hope to the fulfillment of the Lord's promises.

As Mary and Joseph are marveling at his words, Simeon prophesies that Jesus is destined to be the downfall and rise of many and tells Mary, his mother, that her heart will be pierced with a sword—"so that the thoughts of many hearts may be revealed" (Luke 2:34–35). Coming on the scene at this moment is an elderly prophet named Anna, who was always in the temple, calling upon God day and night through prayer and fasting. Anna gave thanks to God and spoke of the child to all who looked forward to the deliverance of Israel (see Luke 2). Her words and actions confirm those of Simeon. Jesus is a child especially blessed and chosen by God for the salvation of his people. As Jesus is presented to God, Simeon and Anna recognize that God is presenting a gift to his people. Jesus, not the temple, will be their means of deliverance.

The sacrifices offered that day are nothing but a vague foreshadowing of Jesus' ultimate sacrifice on the cross at Calvary. Mary ponders what has happened and instinctively understands. Already, her heart is pricked with sorrow.

After they perform their duties, Mary and Joseph return to their own town of Nazareth in Galilee. The ritual observances have been performed: Jesus has been presented to God; Mary has been purified. At Nazareth, the child grows in both size and strength. Wisdom fills his mind, and the grace of God sustains him.

The Mystery of the Presentation reminds us of Israel's longing for the Messiah and her intense desire for salvation. It sees in a small child the culmination of centuries of waiting. It looks upon all Jesus did during his life and ministry as the final outcome of God's ongoing involvement in his people. In this fragile body rest the hopes and dreams of Israel—and all humanity. When we contemplate this Mystery, our own dormant hopes and dreams come alive. We see in this small child the hopes of the past passing through us and moving forward. We see Jesus' parents offering him to God and understand that we must share in a similar offering of self.

Only by offering ourselves to God can we ever hope to share in the blessings of the kingdom. Only by looking beyond our own interests and desires can we discover the meaning of Simeon's words and Anna's prophecy. We are incapable, however, of doing so ourselves. Jesus must encourage us and help us, not once, but time and time again, day after day, for the rest of our lives.

The Mystery of the Presentation teaches us to be more conscious of our own need for purification, our own inner yearning for salvation, and our own dire need for God. It also makes us conscious of our need to recognize God's presence in our lives, especially when we least expect it.

Simeon and Anna were blessed with the gift of recognition. They were able to delve beneath appearances and acknowledge Jesus' true identity. They saw before them not the frail figure of youth, but the Holy One of God, the revealing light of the Gentiles and the glory of Israel. Like them, we too are called to lead holy and pious lives that will help us sense God's presence in our midst. Like them, we must follow the movements of the Spirit in our lives so we will recognize God's words to us and understand their meaning. Like them, we must embrace our inner longing, speak from our hearts, and ponder the reality of God's abiding presence in our midst.

Only then will we be able to follow the path chosen for us by Christ. Only then will his presence within us grow in size and strength and be filled with wisdom. Only then will the grace of God be upon us and lead us to perform wonders—both great and small—for the sake of the kingdom within us and in our midst.

Reflection Questions

- Like Simeon and Anna, are you able to recognize God's presence in your life and in the lives of those around you?
- Are you able to delve beneath appearances and sense God's presence when he passes?
- What do you look for?
- What thoughts has God laid bare for you?
- What dormant hopes and dreams have come alive for you while contemplating his mystery?
- What offering of self has come from them?
- What purification?
- What growth?
- What dedication?
- How have they enabled you to grow in wisdom?

FIFTH JOYFUL MYSTERY

FINDING JESUS IN THE TEMPLE

*Why were you looking for me? Did you not know
that I must be in my Father's house?*

LUKE 2:49

The fifth Joyful Mystery celebrates the finding of the child Jesus in the temple (see Luke 2). As devout and pious Jews, Jesus' parents were accustomed to going to Jerusalem every year for the feast of Passover. On one such occasion, they were making their way back to Nazareth after the feast when they noticed their twelve-year-old son was missing. Since they thought Jesus was in the pilgrimage group, they continued their journey for a day, looking for him among their relatives and friends.

When they failed to find him, however, they quickly returned to Jerusalem and found him on the third day of his disappearance—he was in the temple sitting with the teachers, listening and asking questions. Everyone was amazed at the depth of his wisdom.

Astounded by what they saw, his parents asked him to explain his actions, since they had been searching for him in sorrow for such a long time. Jesus simply replied, "Why were you looking for me? Did you not know that I must be in my Father's house?" Even at this early age, Jesus enjoyed an intimate relationship with the Father and was prepared to share it with those seeking truth.

Aware of his parents' concern for him, Jesus submitted to them as an obedient son and returned with them to Nazareth. Mary, we are told, remembered these incidents from Jesus' childhood. Jesus continued to grow in age, wisdom, and grace before God and men.

For most of his life before the beginning of his public ministry, Jesus is said to have lived a hidden life at Nazareth with his parents, Mary and Joseph. The story of the Finding in the Temple is one of the few scenes from his early life that has made its way into the Gospels. Although the source of this story is undoubtedly Mary, his mother, who is said to have "kept all these things in her heart", the account itself is laden with assertions of faith that make it difficult to distinguish the historical from the theological.

The account appears only in Luke's Gospel and serves as a fitting end to the infancy narrative appearing in the first two chapters. Immediately after this story, Luke takes us into Jesus' baptism in the Jordan and the events of his public ministry.

Luke's story of the Finding of Jesus in the Temple has much to offer. To begin with, it's important to remember that Mary and Joseph take their Son with them to Jerusalem to celebrate Passover, the most important feast on the Jewish calendar. During this time, the Jews celebrate their Exodus from Egypt and their deliverance from slavery. In Jesus' day, the temple in Jerusalem was the center of the Jewish faith, for it housed the Ark of the Covenant and the stone tablets of the Decalogue given to Moses by God atop Mount Sinai.

These religious artifacts symbolized for Israel the essence of God's covenant with them. By placing Jesus in Jerusalem at the time of Passover and having him sit among the learned men of Israel, Luke emphasizes Jesus' reverence for the Law and the Covenant. He also demonstrates the depth of Jesus' wisdom and offers his readers a foreshadowing of the New Passover that will eventually take place through Jesus' passion, death, and resurrection. As the temple of the New Covenant, Jesus is placed in this passage in continuity with Jewish Law and depicted as someone destined to bring it to completion.

The story also has much to tell us about the search for wisdom. Jesus isn't presented as someone whose acquisition of wisdom is complete. Although he impresses with his intelligent answers, he is portrayed primarily as someone eager to listen to learned teachers and ask questions of them. Even when he returns to Nazareth with his parents, he is depicted as someone progressing in "wisdom and age and favor before God" and humanity (Luke 2:52).

Jesus' quest for wisdom involves pondering the depths of the Law and the prophets in the light of his intimate relationship with the Father. He astounds the teachers of the Law (and his parents) because he is learning how to listen to the promptings of the Holy Spirit in his heart.

In doing so, he has tapped into the depths of divine wisdom. At age twelve, Jesus is fast approaching the maturity of insight that will mark his public ministry. Although little is known of his life at Nazareth, the account of the Finding in the Temple reminds us that Jesus' relationship with the Father was carefully nurtured throughout his early life. This event was remembered by Mary and included in Luke's Gospel because it says a great deal about the kind of man Jesus would soon become.

When all is said and done, however, the story of Mary and Joseph's finding Jesus in the temple is probably more about them than Jesus. It's also very much about us. Mary and Joseph cooperated with God in bringing Jesus into the world and were charged with raising him. The story takes place in the context of their annual pilgrimage to Jerusalem. Jesus isn't where his parents expect him to be. Once they locate him, they are astounded by the company he keeps and the wisdom from his lips. Jesus has left them so they can see him in a different light. He stays behind because there is more for him (and them) to learn about his relationship to the Father.

During our own journey through life, we too have been asked to assist in the birth of Jesus. We must allow him to be born within our hearts and do whatever we can to foster his growth and development there. Jesus, however, is not always where we expect to find him, and we can easily lose sight of him.

To rediscover his whereabouts we, like Mary and Joseph, must retrace our steps and look for him with great diligence. Once we find him, we are often surprised by where he has led us and what he is saying to us. We may even be more surprised by what he asks of us.

All of us are called to search for Jesus. All of us are called to find him. All of us are called to journey with him to Nazareth so he can relive his spiritual childhood within us. Only then will his hidden life bear fruit within our hearts. Only then will we advance steadily, like him, in wisdom, age, and grace.

Reflection Questions

- What was your early childhood like?
- Did you know how to listen?
- Did you have a deep desire to learn?
- Did you love and respect God and others?
- Did you thirst for wisdom?
- Were you able to grow in wisdom, age, and grace?
- What about later in life?
- Did you turn around one day and suddenly realize Jesus was missing?
- Did you have to retrace your steps to find him again?
- Were you surprised where you found him?
- Like Mary and Joseph, did you find it difficult to grasp what God was trying to tell you?

PART II

THE LUMINOUS MYSTERIES

The next five Mysteries of the Rosary focus on Jesus' public ministry.

The first decade, the *Baptism of the Lord*, is a prophetic action that marks the transition from Jesus' hidden life at Nazareth to his public life in Galilee and Judea. By receiving the Baptism of John, Jesus embraces the life of repentance it represents and makes it a prerequisite for the baptism of Spirit and fire he has come to bring.

The second decade, his self-manifestation at the *Wedding at Cana,* celebrates his first public miracle. This Mystery asks us to contemplate the power of Jesus to change water into wine as a sign of an even deeper transformation to take place within the human heart.

The third decade, his *Proclamation of the Kingdom of God* and the call to conversion, brings to the fore Jesus' ministry of preaching and teaching. This Mystery highlights Jesus' message that the reign of God is already in our midst and within our hearts.

The fourth decade, the *Transfiguration*, looks at the radiant change in Jesus that took place on a mountaintop in the presence of his closest disciples. This Mystery points beyond Jesus' earthly life to the transformation that would take place at his resurrection.

The fifth decade, the *Institution of the Eucharist*, is a prophetic action that marks the end of Jesus' public ministry and anticipates his passion, death, and resurrection. This Mystery gives us a fore-taste of the messianic banquet and an ongoing testimony of Jesus' presence to the members of his body.

Encompassed by two prophetic actions, these decades of the rosary convey Jesus' public ministry as a cohesive whole. When meditating on these mysteries, we are invited to see them as an integral part of Jesus' life and salvific mission. They highlight both the prophetic and sacramental nature of Jesus' ministry and remind us that this ministry continues to this day in the lives of his followers.

FIRST LUMINOUS MYSTERY

THE BAPTISM OF THE LORD

And a voice came from the heavens,
"You are my beloved Son; with you I am well pleased."
MARK 1:11

The first Luminous Mystery is the Baptism of Jesus, which marked the beginning of Jesus' public ministry. Although Gospel accounts vary in their details of what happened, they concur on one significant point: Jesus was baptized in the Jordan by John. That baptism marked a moment of transition in Jesus' life. His hidden life at Nazareth has come to an end. He has moved into the public forum and will soon choose his first disciples and begin his ministry of teaching and healing.

Christians have long looked upon the Baptist as a precursor of Jesus. He who leapt within Elizabeth's womb at the Visitation is the first to recognize Jesus as "the Lamb of God, who takes away the sin of the world" (John 1:29). He is "the voice of one crying out in the desert, 'Make straight the way of the Lord'" (1:23). He recognizes his place in the divine plan: "I am baptizing you with water, but one mightier than I is coming. I am not worthy to loosen the thongs of his sandals. He will baptize you with the holy Spirit and fire" (Luke 3:16).

John is the last of the Old Testament prophets and the first of the New Testament. He sets the scene for Jesus' appearance on the world stage. He's the first to give public witness that Jesus is "Son of God" (John 1:34) and the first to die for him (see Matthew 14). So closely were their lives and ministries identified with one another that Herod thought Jesus was John the Baptist risen from the dead (see Mark 6:14). John, however, recognized his true relationship with his Lord: "He must increase; I must decrease" (John 3:30).

The Gospels present Jesus' baptism as a prodigious event. In Mark's Gospel, Jesus is said to have come down from Nazareth in Galilee to be baptized by John in the waters of the Jordan. When he comes up out of the water, he immediately sees the sky tearing in two and the Spirit descending on him like a dove. A voice then comes from the heavens: "You are my beloved Son; with you I am well pleased" (Mark 1:9–11).

The Matthew 3 account is similar to Mark's, with one major difference: John at first refuses to baptize Jesus, because John doesn't consider himself worthy to perform such a task. He eventually agrees, however, when Jesus tells him it must be done to fulfill all God demands.

In Luke 3, Jesus' baptism is more public in nature. Many people are baptized that day. After Jesus' baptism, moreover, the opening of the sky, the appearance of the Spirit in the form of a dove, and the voice of divine favor are seen and heard by everyone present.

Although John 1 doesn't make explicit reference to Jesus' baptism by John, it affirms that the Baptist himself saw the Holy Spirit descend upon Jesus to identify him as the One who is to baptize with the Spirit.

Along with the Last Supper, the baptism of Jesus is one of two prophetic actions that encapsulate Jesus' public ministry. These actions are intimately related to the Christ event. Through his baptism in the waters of the Jordan, Jesus immersed himself in and made holy the waters we are immersed in at baptism. His baptism marks the institution of a sacrament of initiation into his paschal mystery.

Water is a symbol of both life and death. By submitting himself to this ritual action at the very beginning of his public ministry, Jesus foreshadows things to come. The waters of the Jordan that cover his body will flow from his pierced side as he hangs dead from the cross.

These same waters cover us at our baptism and immerse us in the mystery of his death. They will also lead us to the empty tomb and a participation in the transformed life of the risen Lord. Baptism makes us members of Christ's body. As such, we are called to carry on his mission of preaching the Good News of the kingdom.

The mystery of the baptism of Jesus invites us to renew our own baptismal vows. Many of us, baptized as infants, are unable to recall our own baptisms. By meditating on Jesus' baptism, we are able to see a reflection of our own and enter into his paschal mystery in a deeply personal way. We listen to our hearts and hear the cry of the Baptist calling us to conversion and the pursuit of holiness. We see in the waters of the Jordan a foreshadowing of the waters of the baptismal font that will immerse us in Christ's death and resurrection and make us members of his Body. We see in the dove appearing over Jesus' head the gift of the Holy Spirit, who washes us clean of sin and makes of our souls a divine dwelling place for the Blessed Trinity. We sense in the voice from heaven both the intimate bond of love between Jesus and his Father and an invitation to enter into it as adopted sons and daughters in a very profound and intimate way.

Jesus' baptism makes possible our own. It frees us from the chains of sin and death and begins in us the process of our own divinization. When Jesus touched the waters of the Jordan, he instituted the sacrament of baptism and sanctified the waters that would eventually flow from a myriad of baptismal fonts dispersed through space and time. When he entered the waters of the Jordan, he was immersed in the reality of his passion and death. When he rose from those same waters, he pulled back the curtain of death and heard the voice of the Father calling him to his right hand.

This action of Christ occurs again and again—at every baptism, regardless of where or when it is performed. It's an action of humility and grace, of courage and strength, of faith and hope, and love. It's an action of Jesus, the Lamb of God, the Anointed One, the Chosen One of God.

After Jesus' baptism, the waters of the Jordan would never again be the same. It is now the largest river in the world, for it flows through the baptismal font of your parish church—and within your very heart.

Reflection Questions

- How is Jesus' baptism related to your own?
- What does it signify?
- To what does it point?
- Has baptism made a difference in your life?
- Would you have been a different person if you had never received it?
- What does it tell you about the reality of sin in your life?
- What does it tell you about repentance and the need for conversion?
- What does it tell you about God's love and the reality of grace?
- What is Jesus saying to you through this sacrament?
- What is he doing to you through this sacrament?
- Is the work complete?

SECOND LUMINOUS MYSTERY

THE WEDDING AT CANA

*Everyone serves good wine first, and then when
people have drunk freely, an inferior one;
but you have kept the good wine until now.*
JOHN 2:10

The second Luminous Mystery involves Jesus' self-manifestation at the Wedding at Cana, where he changed water into wine. The account appears in John 2 and is traditionally considered the first miracle of Jesus' public ministry. In the Gospel of John, it's the first of the "signs" through which Jesus revealed his glory—his relationship to the Father and the power that flows from it—to the world.

By changing water into wine, Jesus demonstrates his command over the elements of nature. This miraculous change points to the eventual transformation of blood and water flowing through the human heart. Jesus manifests himself in this way not to exalt himself but to serve people in need. Jesus' miracles are acts of service.

According to the account in John 2, the miracle takes place on the third day of Jesus' public ministry. In the previous chapter, Jesus spends the first and second days selecting his first disciples. On the third day Jesus, his disciples, and Mary are invited to a wedding feast at the small village of Cana in Galilee. When the wine runs out at a certain point in the celebration, Jesus' mother tells him about it. Jesus asks why it concerns her so and says the time is not ripe for him to reveal himself.

Undaunted by this remark, Mary tells the servants waiting tables to do whatever her son instructs. Nearby, there happened to be six stone jars prescribed for ritual cleansing, each with a capacity of fifteen to twenty-five gallons. Jesus tells the servants to fill the jugs to the brim with water and then draw some out for the waiter in charge. The waiter tastes the water turned to wine and, not knowing where it came from, calls the groom over and remarks that, unlike most hosts who serve the best wine first, he has saved the best for last.

The account ends by reiterating that Jesus performed this first sign at Cana in Galilee, that he revealed his glory through it, and that it led his disciples to believe in him.

The miracle at Cana reveals much about Jesus, his mother, and the call to discipleship. It's no accident that Jesus' first miracle takes place immediately after the call of his first disciples. Part of the reason for this miraculous transformation of water into wine is to reveal his glory and to help his followers to believe in him.

As one might expect, his mother has already traveled this road and has no need of any miraculous sign or display of power. She is responding to a real need in the life of a newly married couple. They've run out of wine at their wedding feast and have no idea what to do. Seeing their predicament, Mary informs her son of the difficulty. Jesus seems hesitant at first, for his hour has not yet come, but he responds to the need in a quiet yet incredible display of power.

The point of this part of the story couldn't be any clearer. Mary intercedes with her son for those in need. He, in turn, listens to his mother's requests, granting them even when the request is inopportune or the moment not right. He does so because of his love for his mother and his own sensitivity to the needs of the present moment.

Mary has often been described as the Christian disciple *par excellence.* Her faith in her son and her humble request inspire him to perform his first miracle. She herself, however, works behind the scenes in a simple and quiet way. She doesn't wish to draw attention to herself, but to allow the newly married couple's celebration to continue without interruption or embarrassment. Her faith in Christ causes him to act in the lives of others. Ultimately, it brings the disciples themselves to believe in him more deeply.

Once again, the point couldn't be clearer. Mary's role in the work of salvation is to intercede for us and lead us to Christ. She works with her son to bring him to others. If we turn to Mary with our needs, they ultimately will be presented to Christ. As in the case of the newly married couple at Cana, our needs are often looked after by Mary and her son even before we ask for help. Mary and Jesus are our friends; they actively seek our well-being in all times, places, and circumstances.

We should note, moreover, that Jesus doesn't merely turn water into wine at the Wedding at Cana. He produces the *very best* wine for the occasion, the kind that should be served at the beginning of the celebration when those invited can properly discern the quality of drink being served them.

We can garner an important message from this small detail. Jesus doesn't skimp. His love for us is plentiful, and he works on our behalf in a bountiful way. We shouldn't be afraid, therefore, to bring our needs to Jesus and his mother. And we shouldn't expect him to hold back in lavishing his gifts and treasures upon us.

Like the disciples who accompanied him to the wedding feast, Jesus calls us by name and asks us to follow him. If we do so, he promises, there is nothing for us to worry about, for he will watch over us and provide for our every need. He will do so, moreover, in abundance and with the best of quality.

Jesus' first miracle reminds us we have no need too small or too large for him. It encourages us to invite him and his mother to participate in our celebration of life and to allow them to roam the courtyards and inner rooms of the banquet hall of our hearts. If we grant them entrance, they'll take it upon themselves to look after our needs and replenish our spirits beyond our wildest expectations. The miracles they perform there will far exceed anything the Gospels themselves have recounted. They'll transform our stony hearts into fleshy hearts and allow the Spirit of God himself to enter there and dwell within us.

Reflection Questions

- Has Jesus performed any signs for you to help you to believe?
- How has he revealed his glory to you?
- How has he taken care of your needs?
- What role has Mary played in these actions?
- Has she taken notice of your needs and brought them to her son?
- Has she helped you along in the walk of discipleship?
- Have you invited Jesus and Mary to join you in your celebration of life?
- Have you granted them entrance into the banquet hall of your heart?
- What is keeping you from doing so?

THIRD LUMINOUS MYSTERY

THE PROCLAMATION OF THE KINGDOM OF GOD

This is the time of fulfillment. The kingdom of God is
at hand. Repent, and believe in the gospel.
MARK 1:15

The third Luminous Mystery concerns Jesus' call to conversion. His public ministry was marked by his preaching of the nearness of the kingdom. A sense of urgency accompanies his actions. Everything he says and does points to the imminent coming of God's reign. Jesus conveys his message through simple words and parables, using examples from everyday life to challenge our perceptions and force us to choose between self-centeredness and God-centeredness.

We opt for the first by always putting ourselves first in the path we forge through life. We select the second by giving God and others primacy of place. Jesus has come to remind us of the urgency of this choice. The time is now for us to reform our lives and believe the Gospel. Unlike many of the other Mysteries of the rosary, Jesus' Proclamation of the Kingdom isn't confined to a single account from Scripture. His preaching on God's reign permeates the Gospel narratives. When meditating upon this Mystery, therefore, we are drawn not to one, but to a variety of texts.

Each of his parables, for example, contains a message about the kingdom. Typical of these is the parable of the mustard seed (see Mark 4:30–32, Matthew 13:31–32, and Luke 13:18–19), where the kingdom of God is likened to a tiny seed that grows into the largest of shrubs. Like that seed, the kingdom has its roots in humble beginnings but will develop in time beyond expectations.

Other typical parables of the kingdom are about the treasure and the pearl (see Matthew 13:44–46). In these parables, the kingdom is likened to something of great value that causes us to risk everything to get it.

Yet another parable of the kingdom is the one about the prodigal son (see Luke 15:11–32), where relationships in the kingdom are centered on forgiveness and the love of the Father.

Each parable concentrates on a specific aspect of the kingdom. Any could be used for meditation on Jesus' message.

Another place Jesus gives prominence to the Proclamation of the Kingdom and the call to conversion are "The Sermon on the Mount" (see Matthew 5—7) and "The Sermon on the Plain" (see Luke 6:17–49). Here Jesus presents the values of the kingdom. Most representative of these values are the beatitudes (see Matthew 5:3–12; Luke 6:20–26), a series of blessings upon the poor and oppressed in which Jesus presents a vision of those destined to be citizens of his kingdom: The poor shall be in possession of God's reign; the hungry shall have their fill; those who weep shall laugh; those who are persecuted for his sake shall rejoice in the kingdom of heaven.

Throughout his proclamation of the kingdom, Jesus is always on the side of the poor and powerless. He states this explicitly in Luke 4:16–22, when he announces at synagogue that he has come to fulfill the words of the prophet Isaiah: "The Spirit of the Lord is upon me, because he has anointed me to bring glad tidings to the poor. He has sent me to proclaim liberty to captives and recovery of sight to the blind, to let the oppressed go free, and to proclaim a year acceptable to the Lord."

As this account indicates, Jesus spoke with wisdom and authority. Those who heard him knew that he spoke from the depths of his heart and from a deep experience of the Spirit of God in his life. It was because he spoke with such authority that his message penetrated the hearts of his hearers and took root.

Jesus' proclamation of the kingdom and the call to conversion is probably best exemplified when he teaches his disciples how to pray (see Luke 11 and Matthew 6). The Our Father is considered the Christian prayer *par excellence.*

The first part of the prayer addresses the Father with words of praise and adoration: "Our Father in heaven, hallowed be your name, your kingdom come, your will be done, on earth as in heaven."

The second part of the prayer is a series of petitions bringing to the Father our most basic of needs: "Give us today our daily bread; and forgive us our debts, as we forgive our debtors; and do not subject us to the final test, but deliver us from the evil one."

Both parts of the prayer speak of the kingdom. The first part identifies the kingdom closely with doing the Father's will; the second focuses on forgiveness as key to entering the kingdom. Together they represent a desire to give honor and glory to the Father and to make present in this life the values of the kingdom to come.

By inviting us to meditate on Jesus' proclamation of the kingdom and its accompanying call to conversion, this Mystery of the Rosary asks us to discover the relevance of this message for our lives today. It bids us to examine the values that shape our lives and judge them against those preached by Christ. These are expressed most clearly in the words of love he left us in John 15: "As the Father loves me, so I also love you. Remain in my love" (verse 9). "No one has greater love than this, to lay down one's life for one's friends" (13). "This I command you: love one another" (17).

Jesus' proclamation of the kingdom is a proclamation of God's love for us. His call to conversion is to open our hearts so we will love God with all our heart, soul, mind, and strength—and will love our neighbors as ourselves (see Mark 12:29–31).

When we meditate on this Mystery, we come to see that we share in Jesus' proclamation of the kingdom through the love we share. The more we love, the more the kingdom becomes present in our midst. The more we love, the further along the road of conversion we travel. The more we love, the closer we come to God, to one another, and to our very selves.

Reflection Questions

- How do you proclaim Jesus' message of love and forgiveness?
- Do you find it easy or difficult?
- Where do you turn for help?
- Are any of Jesus' words particularly helpful?
- Do you read them often?
- Who are the poor and powerless in your life?
- How do you relate to them?
- How would Jesus want you to relate to them?
- Is there anything in that relationship in need of change?
- What does it mean to pray for the coming of the kingdom?

FOURTH LUMINOUS MYSTERY

THE TRANSFIGURATION

He was transfigured before them, and his clothes became
dazzling white, such as no fuller on earth could bleach them.
MARK 9:2–3

The fourth Luminous Mystery is the Transfiguration, accounts of which appear in the Gospels of Matthew (17:1–8), Mark (9:2–8), and Luke (9:28–36). Although these accounts differ in subtle ways, they all use standard narrative techniques to draw a close connection between Jesus' transfigured state and the life of discipleship. In a way, they say as much about the deepest hopes of those who accompany Jesus on the mountain of transfiguration as they do about Jesus himself.

The plot is fundamentally the same in all three accounts. Jesus leads Peter, James, and John up a high mountain. When they reach the top, he is transfigured before their very eyes, so much so that his clothes become dazzling white. Elijah and Moses appear and engage Jesus in conversation. The three disciples are overcome with awe. Peter speaks up and tells Jesus how good it is for them to be there. Beside himself and hardly knowing what to say, he suggests building three booths on the site: one for Jesus, one for Elijah, and one for Moses.

At that moment, a cloud overshadows them. Out of the cloud comes a voice identifying Jesus as a beloved Son and telling the disciples to listen to him. When the cloud passes, the disciples look around and see no one with them but Jesus. The disciples tell no one what they saw.

Jesus' transfiguration reveals his glory as no other incident in his public life does. His disciples not only witness a dazzling change in Jesus' features before their very eyes, but also see him conversing with two of the greatest figures of the Old Testament. Moses and Elijah represent the Law and the Prophets, the two major features of the Hebrew Scriptures. That Jesus stands with them demonstrates his continuity with God's revelation to the Jews.

One might wonder what the three figures are talking about. Matthew and Mark are silent on this matter. Luke's account, however, says they spoke of Jesus' passage, which he was about to fulfill in Jerusalem (see Luke 9:31). "Fulfillment" implies that Jesus' passage in Jerusalem is somehow foreshadowed in the Law and the Prophets. Jesus is thus represented as the culmination of all that has been revealed through the Law and the Prophets. The voice from the cloud verifies this claim by identifying Jesus as God's beloved Son and Chosen One.

The juxtaposition of an event revealing Jesus' glory with a conversation relating to his passion and death points to the even deeper revelation of Jesus' glory that will take place in the resurrection. It's no small matter that this foreshadowing of the resurrection is given to Jesus' closest disciples.

The transfiguration of Jesus foreshadows his resurrection, gives his disciples an experiential glimpse into the transformation of life each of them will hope one day to fully enjoy, and tells us something about the final transformation of human existence.

Jesus ascends a mountain in the company of his closest disciples. Before their very eyes, he is bodily transfigured, engages the Law and the Prophets in conversation, and receives a spiritual blessing from his Father in heaven.

The disciples, in turn, are overcome by an experience of awe and are strictly enjoined not to tell anyone what they've seen until the Son of Man rises from the dead. When taken together, these diverse elements show that, as a foreshadowing of the resurrection, Jesus' transfiguration has bodily, emotional, intellectual, spiritual, and even social dimensions to it. It points to the transformation of the whole person and reminds us that our deepest hopes are anticipated and fulfilled by Jesus.

The transfiguration narrative reminds us 1) that salvation comes from the power of Jesus' death and resurrection and 2) that the true disciple wishes always to remain with Jesus and follow him wherever he leads. As a christological event, the transfiguration prefigures Jesus' resurrection and our own participation in it as members of his Body.

The religious experience of the disciples also needs mentioning. Mountaintops often serve as a locus for a meeting between the human and divine. Peter, James, and John's experience of Jesus on the mountain filled them with awe, deepened their desire to remain with their Master, and increased their sense of the need to listen to him. Genuine religious experience involves elements of awe, communion, and listening. For Christians, it entails a personal encounter with Jesus Christ, the Word made flesh, who translates the mysteries of the Father for the limited capacities of human experience.

Jesus' transfiguration encourages us to reflect on the meaning of our own "peak" religious experiences. When have we experienced the depths of religious awe in our lives? To what extent do we think of ourselves as "keeping company" with the Lord? How do we listen to the Lord? How do we respond to those words? When in our lives have we felt particularly close to God, and when have the elements of awe, communion, and listening had special relevance?

Moments of transfiguration occur wherever these three elements converge. They point to the lingering need all Christians have to live the Gospel message on deep level of consciousness.

Reflection Questions

- Can you point to a specific moment in your life when you had a deeply personal religious experience?
- If so, what effect did that experience have on you?
- What did you learn about God from it?
- What did you learn about others?
- What did you learn about yourself?
- Where did that experience take you?
- How did it change your life?
- If you've never had such an experience, can you picture Jesus going up the mountain along with his closest disciples?
- Can you ask him if you can accompany him?
- What is preventing you from doing so?

FIFTH LUMINOUS MYSTERY

THE INSTITUTION OF THE EUCHARIST

While they were eating, Jesus took bread,
said the blessing, broke it, and giving it to his disciples
said, "Take and eat; this is my body."
MATTHEW 26:26

The fifth Luminous Mystery is the Institution of the Eucharist at the Last Supper. The Eucharist is the center of the Christian community. It gives its members the strength and endurance to overcome areas of their lives in which they've weakened and given in to the impulses of the flesh.

Division in the eucharistic assembly is a clear sign that the community is veering away from the love of Christ. Only by restoring that intrinsic unity to the life of the community will there be hope for the other external divisions to be bound up and eventually healed.

The earliest account of Jesus' Institution of the Eucharist comes in Saint Paul's First Letter to the Corinthians: "I received from the Lord what I also handed on to you, that the Lord Jesus, on the night he was handed over, took bread, and, after he had given thanks, broke it and said, 'This is my body that is for you. Do this in remembrance of me.'" In the same way also the cup, after supper, saying, 'This cup is the new covenant in my blood. Do this, as often as you drink it, in remembrance of me'"(11:23–25).

For centuries, Christians have defined themselves by this simple ritual of breaking bread together and passing the cup. The Eucharist is where they go to renew themselves spiritually.

In its reflection on the meaning of the Eucharist, the Church identifies three key themes. First, the eucharistic action is a proclamation of the death of the Lord Jesus. This *sacrificial* dimension of the Eucharist comes directly from words of Jesus describing the cup as the "new covenant" in his blood, a reference to the ancient practice of spilling the blood of sacrificial animals to both seal and renew a sacred bond between God and men. The Lord's Supper is a proclamation of Jesus' sacrificial offering. His blood was shed on the cross so a new covenant between God and humanity could be established for all time. To eat the Body and to drink the Blood of the Lord is to affirm one's faith in Christ's sacrificial death for the sins of the world. It's a proclamation of a new bond between the human and the divine, a bond that cannot be broken—not even by death itself.

The second theme is that the eucharistic action actually brings about the *presence* of Jesus in the bread and wine itself as well as in the believing community. To not recognize Jesus in the Body is to bring judgment upon oneself. To treat fellow Christians in such an irreverent way is to act in similar fashion toward the Lord himself. The close bond between the presence of Christ in the bread and wine and the presence of Christ in the believing community is something to be carefully guarded and deeply cherished. This is why Jesus is so deeply concerned that the eucharistic assembly should be imbued with a spirit of generosity and heartfelt love.

Finally, the eucharistic action points to the *banquet* in the kingdom that is to come. The Eucharist takes place in the present, looks to the past, but is intrinsically directed toward the fulfillment of Christ's promises that will come about at his *Parousia* or Second Coming. This eschatological orientation of the eucharistic action reminds us that our present time-bound existence will one day overflow into the eternal fullness of God's endearing love. The coming of the Lord Jesus is heralded by the eucharistic action of the believing community, which looks with expectant hope for the definitive rule of God's reign in the hearts of men.

Unity in belief and liturgical practice is an essential ingredient of the vibrant Christian community. Lack of unity generally disrupts the movement of the Spirit within the community and its members and hinders its missionary witness to the world beyond. It sets one member of the Body against the other, thus preventing members from working together for the sake of the kingdom. The unity in Christ's Body must be affirmed as an underlying reality and a goal to be constantly striven for. The unity of the believing community is a reality caused by Christ by virtue of his sacrificial death—and a reality continuously sought by his disciples in anticipation of his return.

Today, local Christian communities are often burdened by divisive tensions that weigh them down and prevent them from giving witness to the vibrant presence of the Gospel message in their lives. Whatever the cause of such divisions (personality clashes, divergent theological opinions, questions of power and authority), we need to examine ourselves to see if our actions correspond to what we profess when we participate in the Eucharist and receive the Body and Blood of Christ.

Deep dissension within a local community is nearly always a sign that the Body of Christ is not receiving the reverence and respect it deserves. The presence of Christ in the Eucharist and in his Body, the Church, are so deeply intertwined that divisions within community can only be accounted for by a failure to recognize the true significance of the action of Christ taking place in the Eucharist. The gap between what the Eucharist causes and how community members behave toward one another has no other feasible explanation.

To one extent or another, every Christian community has its share of internal division and disrupting, factious behavior. The eschatological dimension of the eucharistic celebration itself reminds us that our pilgrimage through time isn't over and that as long as it continues, a gap is almost sure to exist between the ideals we profess and the concrete behavior exhibited in our lives.

When seen in this light, the question we face when dealing with such internal tensions is whether the gap between faith and practice in our daily lives is getting larger or smaller. The response to this question will have a great influence on how we perceive ourselves as a community and what concrete steps should be taken to ensure the community's faithfulness to the Gospel and a life of ongoing conversion.

Reflection Questions

- Do you understand the Eucharist more as a banquet, presence, or sacrifice?
- Do you have a difficult time understanding any of these dimensions of the sacrament?
- Do you have a difficult time accepting any of them?
- Which, for you, is the easiest to accept?
- Which is the most difficult?
- In what way is the Eucharist a source of unity for Christians?
- In what way is the Eucharist a source of disunity?
- What concrete steps can you take in your local community to heal internal tensions and bring people around the table of the Lord?

PART III

THE SORROWFUL MYSTERIES

The next five Mysteries of the Rosary concern the horrific events of Jesus' passion and death. They lead us through the drama of Calvary, which began the night before he died and culminated atop the small hill outside the Gate of Jerusalem known as *Golgotha*, "The Place of the Skull."

The first decade, *Jesus' Agony in the Garden of Gethsemane*, depicts Jesus' intense internal suffering over his impending death and his struggle to do his Father's will regardless of where it leads.

The second decade, the *Scourging at the Pillar*, shows the humiliation he went through when the soldiers stripped him of his garments and savagely beat him. It highlights the physical and psychological degradation he freely embraced out of love for us.

The third decade, the *Crowning With Thorns*, shows how the soldiers ridiculed him by dressing him in a purple cloak, placing a makeshift crown on his head, and hailing him as King of the Jews. It reminds us Jesus' kingdom is not of this world and of what membership in that kingdom entails.

The fourth decade, the *Carrying of the Cross*, presents the way of Calvary. It reminds us of what Jesus went through before his death and what we also must endure if we wish to follow him.

The fifth decade, the *Crucifixion*, presents Jesus' death on the cross. It confronts us with the mystery of Jesus' death and bids us to see in it the means of our salvation.

Each Mystery builds on the one before it and culminates in Jesus horrible death atop Golgotha. Taken together, they remind us of the suffering Jesus underwent for our sake and of the path each of us must also walk for the sake of the kingdom.

FIRST SORROWFUL MYSTERY

JESUS' AGONY IN THE GARDEN OF GETHSEMANE

Father, if you are willing, take this cup away from me;
still, not my will but yours be done.
LUKE 22:42

The first Sorrowful Mystery is the agony in the garden of Gethsemane (see Matthew 26:36–47, Mark 14:32–42; Luke 22:40–46; John 18:1). Although the accounts differ in details, all agree that Jesus went to the garden with his disciples to pray and was there taken under arrest.

Mark 14 presents the earliest narrative of the event. After his Last Supper, Jesus goes with his disciples to a place called Gethsemane and asks them to sit down while he goes off to pray, taking Peter, James, and John with him.

He begins to be filled with fear and distress and tells the three disciples that his heart is filled with sorrow to the point of death. He asks them to stay behind and remain awake. Advancing a little further, Jesus falls to the ground and prays for this hour to pass him by. He addresses God as "Abba, Father," who has the power to do all things, and begs him to take the approaching cup of suffering away from him. In the end, however, he asks for things to go according to his Father's will, not his.

Finding Peter, James, and John asleep at his return, Jesus wakes them and asks Peter why he couldn't stay awake even for a single hour. He tells him to be on guard and to pray not to be put to the test, for "the spirit is willing but the flesh is weak."

Jesus goes off to pray in the same way for a second time and then for a third time. Each time he returns, he finds the three disciples asleep. They cannot keep their eyes open and don't know what to say to Jesus. The third time, he says to them, "Are you still sleeping and taking your rest? Behold, the hour is at hand when the Son of Man is to be handed over to sinners. Get up, let us go. Look, my betrayer is at hand." At that moment, Judas comes with a crowd armed with swords and clubs to seize him and take him to the Sanhedrin.

Jesus' Agony in the Garden presents a powerful account of the intense inner suffering he went through before his trial and death by crucifixion. Scripture affirms that he was like us in all things but sin (see Hebrews 2:17 and 4:15). At Gethsemane, Jesus plumbs the depths of human fear and anxiety. He knows he's going to die a violent death and that he will ultimately have to face it alone.

As his end draws near, the reality of what he must soon undergo becomes overwhelming. His heart becomes so heavy with sorrow that he feels he will die from it. Jesus, however, doesn't run away from his agony; he brings it instead to his Father in prayer. After throwing himself to the ground, he calls upon "Abba," his Father in heaven, and asks him to allow this cup of suffering to pass. He acknowledges the depths of his inner fears and anxieties to God.

Sharing this inner turmoil with his Father strengthens him and enables him to find the words that have come to characterize his entire life: "I will but what you will" (Mark 14:36). By turning to the Father in prayer, Jesus receives the courage and strength to carry on. Even when he finds his closest disciples asleep at their posts, he doesn't despair, but returns to the Father in prayer again and again until the hour of his betrayal is upon him.

Jesus' disciples don't understand what Jesus is going through; rather than staying awake and keeping vigil, they succumb to sleep, possibly from the lateness of the hour and the effects of the big meal they have just eaten with their master. Whatever the case, they fail to carry out the one request Jesus makes of them—to stay awake while he goes off to pray.

It's noteworthy that the three disciples Jesus singles out to come with him—Peter, James, and John—are those who, early on in his public ministry, accompanied him up the mountain to witness his Transfiguration (see Mark 9:2–13). Having witnessed his majesty and glory, perhaps they feel there is nothing to worry about and that nothing could ever happen to Jesus. Perhaps they have forgotten—or never fully understood—what Jesus told them as they descended the mountain about the suffering the Son of Man must endure (Mark 9:12). Perhaps they're overcome with fear and anxiety but, unlike Jesus, are paralyzed and lulled by their depression into a deep melancholic sleep. Whatever the cause, Jesus' closest disciples are not present to him during one of the most painful and critical moments of his life. As Jesus' arrest takes place, it is not surprising that even his closest disciples would desert him and flee (Mark 14:50).

Jesus' agony in the Garden of Gethsemane teaches us a great deal about how we should deal with our own fears and anxieties. Like Jesus, we will sometimes be overwhelmed by intense inner suffering. Sorrow and melancholy fill our hearts, and we seek ways to escape the inevitable. Some of us may even become paralyzed by what we are experiencing and be unable to act effectively.

Jesus teaches that in times of great distress, the most important thing we can do is to share our fears and anxieties honestly with God in prayer. By opening our hearts to God and allowing him to see what we're going through, we find him opening his own heart to us. By communing with him in this way, we soon find ourselves expressing our needs to him and ultimately asking that all be done according to his will, not ours.

Unfortunately, like the disciples in the Gospel scene, most of us find it difficult to carry out even the simplest of Jesus' requests. We fail to stay awake spiritually and thus cannot see how prayer can help us in times of difficulty. We look for more pragmatic solutions—we simply fall asleep.

This Mystery of the Rosary invites us to rediscover the intimate relationship we can have with God. It reminds us that true courage and strength come from our relationship with the Father, a bond nourished and strengthened by an intimate life of heartfelt prayer. When we meditate on this Mystery of the Rosary, we come to see that Jesus has plumbed the depths of human suffering and that it was his deep bond of love for "Abba," his Father, that enabled him to continue.

In one way or another, the garden of Gethsemane awaits us all. We hope that when we enter it, it will be a time of deep soul-searching and heart-rending prayer to the Father. If we fall asleep, we have no one to blame but ourselves.

Reflection Questions

- How do you deal with intense internal suffering? Repress it? Run away from it? Stare it in the face? Share it with others? Share it with God?
- How did Jesus deal with it?
- Can you see yourself doing the same?
- Do you share your fear and distress with God?
- Do you open your heart to him in prayer and show him everything?
- Do you know how and when to do so?
- What will your Garden of Gethsemane be like?
- Are your prepared to face it?
- Is it already upon you?

SECOND SORROWFUL MYSTERY

THE SCOURGING AT THE PILLAR

Then Pilate took Jesus and had him scourged.
JOHN 19:1

The second Sorrowful Mystery is the scourging at the pillar. References to this scourging appear in all four Gospel narratives (see Matthew 27; Mark 15; Luke 23; John 19).

After his arrest, Jesus is taken to the Sanhedrin to be interrogated by Jewish religious leaders and then to Pontius Pilate, the Roman governor of Palestine. In some accounts, Pilate sends Jesus to Herod, under whose jurisdiction Galilee fell and who happened to be in Jerusalem for the holy days. Herod interrogates Jesus at length before sending him back to Pilate to decide his fate.

At first, Pilate wishes to release Jesus, for he can find no case against him. In the Gospel of John, the scourging is presented as a lesser penalty inflicted on Jesus by Pilate to gain the crowd's sympathy and Jesus' eventual release. Some of the other Gospels present the scourging as a preliminary stage of death by crucifixion.

Regardless of Pilate's attitude toward Jesus, unrest in the crowd seems to have propelled him into dealing with Jesus as expediently as possible. When the unruly crowd keeps calling for Jesus' execution and, as some accounts suggest, even chooses the release of hardened-criminal Barabbas over Jesus, Pilate washes his hands of the matter and orders Jesus' crucifixion.

Death by crucifixion was a slow, tortuous process which, according to Roman practice, normally began by stripping the criminal and scourging him at the place of judgment to publicly humiliate the criminal and to sap his strength so his death wouldn't take too long and thus inconvenience his executioners. The aim of scourging was to inflict as much psychological and physical injury as possible without weakening the prisoner so much that he wouldn't be able to carry his crossbeam through the streets to his place of execution.

The scourging was normally limited to thirty-nine lashes, although Roman executioners had a reputation for brutality and were known to go beyond that number. The whips were leather thongs with small pieces of bone or metal tied to the ends that would bite into the skin and draw blood.

Jesus, it seems, was weakened considerably by his scourging, for tradition has it that he fell three times as he carried his cross through the streets of Jerusalem to the place of execution, a small hill outside the gates of the city known as Golgotha, "The Place of the Skull." To prevent his premature death, the Romans enlisted the help of an onlooker to bear Jesus' load. The Romans weren't acting mercifully; they were simply trying to ensure that Jesus would stay alive long enough to experience the full weight of his death sentence. By all accounts, they performed this task exceedingly well.

When meditating on this Mystery of the Rosary we are immediately struck by the humiliation to which Jesus was subjected. He was stripped naked when he received the flogging, although he was probably given back his clothing after his scourging (a concession the Romans grudgingly gave to the Jews at public executions). The scourging most likely took place out of the public eye so the Roman soldiers could take liberties with the prescribed orders.

One can only guess at the extent of Jesus' physical wounds. The scourging didn't kill him, but it most certainly drained him of his physical strength. Had nothing else been done to him, the scourging itself probably would have taken his life. As it turns out, it was only the first of a series of mental and physical torments he would be forced to undergo.

This Mystery of the Rosary also reveals something about ourselves. Like the angry crowd, we often prejudge others and demand the harshest of penalties. We give in easily to group pressure and are unable to make impartial judgments about life-and-death issues. Like Pilate, many of us like to take the easy way out. Rather than acting out of our beliefs and convictions, we often choose the action that will calm the anger of others and cause the least amount of trouble. Rather than speaking up and intervening in a situation, we wash our hands of it and allow events to play themselves out without our own active input. Like the soldiers, we can inflict terrible wounds on others as a result of our own brutality and insensitivity. We use words, thoughts, and actions to tear others down rather than build them up. We fail to see, moreover, that when we inflict these brutal and senseless wounds on others, we also harm Christ and, ultimately, ourselves. Our sins against God and others represent a debasing of our own human dignity.

At other times, like Jesus, we are the victims of the brutality and insensitivity of others. We become the objects of public scorn and feel utterly humiliated by the way others treat us. We become deeply wounded by this hateful treatment and feel helpless and at a loss about what to do. Like Jesus, we feel as though we've been tied to the pillar and can do nothing but put up with the cruelty and hatred that has been unjustly directed toward us. Worse yet, the torments we receive may be only the beginning of a long line of insults and injuries. Jesus' scourging at the pillar invites us to unite our suffering with his. It reminds us that our fate is intimately bound with his and that the suffering we undergo is somehow connected to his own.

This Mystery of the Rosary invites us to take a deeper look at the presence of suffering in our lives and to recommit ourselves to following Jesus even through the most intense and difficult moments of his passion. It asks us to meditate on his suffering and to find there a reflection of our own—and that of all humanity.

Reflection Questions

- Which characters in the account of Jesus' scourging do you identify with most? With the crowd, which prejudged Jesus and demanded the harshest penalties for him? With Pilate, who took the easy way out? With the soldiers, who inflicted terrible wounds on Jesus as a result of their brutality and insensitivity? Or with Jesus, who was the object of public scorn and the victim of unqualified hatred?
- With which characters do you identify the least?
- Have you ever felt like both the victim *and* the victimizer?
- How does the account of Jesus' scourging at the pillar help you deal with your experiences of suffering and humiliation?

THIRD SORROWFUL MYSTERY

THE CROWNING WITH THORNS

And the soldiers wove a crown out of thorns
and placed it on his head,
and clothed him in a purple cloak.
JOHN 19:2

The third Sorrowful Mystery is the crowning with thorns. Reference to this mock coronation appears in three of the Gospels (Matthew 27:27–31; Mark 15:16–20; John 19:1–5). Although Luke's Gospel makes no explicit reference to a crown of thorns, it does say that Herod and his guards treated Jesus with contempt before sending him back to Pilate draped in a magnificent robe (Luke 23:11).

Apparently Jesus' claim to kingship caused much laughter among his captors, and physically mistreating Jesus wasn't enough. After the scourging, they further humiliated him by subjecting him to their excessive taunts and jeers.

The ritual was most likely conceived and executed by the Roman soldiers responsible for guarding Jesus. They not only flogged him at Pilate's request, but also ridiculed him for his outlandish claims. Jesus, we should recall, didn't deny he was a king when asked by Pilate (John 18:36–37). When the soldiers had him completely in their charge, they placed a crown of thorns on his head, put a cloak of royal purple around his shoulders, and slapped him, saying, "Hail, King of the Jews!" Some accounts say they put a reed in his right hand and genuflected before him as they pretended to pay homage to him. They also spat at him and hit him on the head with the reed he was holding.

The soldiers' intent was to make a complete and utter fool of Jesus. After they had their fun with him, they redressed him and took him off for crucifixion. The crown of thorns remained on his head throughout his execution. The soldiers' joke received official status through the inscription on the cross outlining the charge against Jesus: "This is Jesus, the King of the Jews" (Matthew 27:37; also see Mark 15:26; Luke 23:38; John 19:19).

Jesus' mock coronation is about power, cruelty, and unbelief. A king has power and authority. To the soldiers, Jesus had none of these. He could do nothing to stop their taunts and humiliating jeers but submit to their power and authority. The soldiers wielded their power over Jesus in the most brutal and barbaric ways.

Jesus was tried for claiming to be a king. He had no soldiers or cohorts to carry out his commands. He had no personal bodyguards to protect him from the soldiers' insulting blows. He stood naked and completely powerless before his executioners. He received their blows in silence and would forgive them from the cross for their ignorance.

The soldiers acted this way because they didn't have the slightest clue about Jesus' identity. All they were able to see was a pathetic, broken man. They couldn't believe his claims because they didn't have hard evidence to fall back on. And so they added mockery to scorn. They crowned him and give him a scepter, but treated him in a most brutal and ignoble manner. They laughed at him, spat at him, slapped him around, and pretended to pay homage to him.

As we meditate on this Mystery of the Rosary, we should ask ourselves if we are much different from those who mocked Jesus on the day of his death. We may call ourselves his disciples, but do we not make a mockery and sham of him through the insensitive (and often brutal) ways we treat others?

Jesus left us with a simple command: to love one another (see John 15:17). How can we call him our Lord and Master when we harbor grudges and refuse to forgive those who have hurt us? Do we not mock him when we pay someone back for their unkindness to us with a cold stare or by ignoring their presence? Do we not belittle his teaching when we genuflect before his tabernacle at church, yet refuse to honor his presence in those around us?

Through the centuries, Christians have found all kinds of ways to mock Jesus. We are no exception. We may not crown him with thorns and openly ridicule him like the Roman soldiers. Our methods are much more subtle. Because we call ourselves Christians, however, our mockery of Jesus is much more hurtful and damaging.

Through it all, Jesus receives our taunts and forgives us, even when we don't explicitly ask for it. He knows what it's like to be betrayed and forsaken by those he loves. He also knows what it's like to be mocked and ridiculed by them. Jesus looks through all of our cruelty and unbelief. He peers into our hearts and sees what we can become through the power of his transforming love. He sees that power already at work in some small corner of our hearts and waits patiently for it to grow.

Jesus also sees himself in our hearts. He sees us struggling to love, trying to forgive, and wanting to be able to turn the other cheek. He sees himself in us when we are mocked and ridiculed by others for our beliefs. He is with us when we're scorned and looked down on, when we're insulted and made fun of.

Although Jesus has already gone through his mock coronation, he lives through it again through the members of his Body. We are the ones who carry the presence of Jesus to the world today. And today, as in Jesus' day, the world doesn't understand who he is. Because we are trying to follow him, we too are not understood by others and at times are mocked and scorned—even persecuted. Through it all, Jesus promises to be with us and bless us.

The words he spoke on the mountainside so many years ago have special significance for all who courageously seek to follow him in times of trial and distress: "Blessed are you when they insult you and persecute you and utter every kind of evil against you (falsely) because of me. Rejoice and be glad, for your reward will be great in heaven. Thus they persecuted the prophets who were before you" (Matthew 5:11–12).

Reflection Questions

- Have you ever been the subject of taunts and laughter?
- How did you respond?
- Do you think you responded in the right way?
- What else could you have done?
- How did Jesus respond?
- Can you see yourself acting in the same way?
- What would it take to do so?
- Have you ever mocked another person?
- Have you ever joined others who were doing so?
- How did you make that person feel?
- Why did you do it?
- Do you think you could have restrained yourself?
- Why didn't you?

FOURTH SORROWFUL MYSTERY

CARRYING OF THE CROSS

*Then he handed him over to them to be
crucified. So they took Jesus, and carrying the
cross himself he went out to what is called
the Place of the Skull, in Hebrew, Golgotha.*
JOHN 19:16–17

After the scourging and mock coronation at the hands of the Roman soldiers, Jesus was led to his place of execution. Crucifixion
by the Romans began with stripping and scourging the criminal
at the place of judgment. To shame him before the people even
further, he was forced to carry the crossbeam through the streets
to the place of execution. He was mocked and often spat upon by
those who lined the streets. If his strength appeared to be waning,
someone was forced to carry the crossbeam for him so he wouldn't
die before he reached the place of execution.

The Gospels give specific details about Jesus' walk from his place
of judgment, *Gabbatha* ("Stone Pavement"; John 19), to his place
of execution, *Golgotha* ("Place of the Skull"), a small hill outside
the city gates. First, we are told that the Romans enlisted a passerby
named Simon of Cyrene to help Jesus carry his cross (Matthew
27). Some Gospels say the Romans encountered this man as he
was coming in from the fields (Mark 15; Luke 23). Luke's Gospel
adds that he was made to carry the crossbeam behind Jesus. Mark's
Gospel says that Simon of Cyrene was the father of Alexander and
Rufus, an indication that his family was known to the early Christian community and possibly had become believers themselves.

Although John's Gospel makes no mention of Simon, Jesus was most likely too weak from his scourging to carry his cross unaided through the narrow winding streets of Jerusalem and outside the city gates to his place of execution. In giving Jesus this help, however, the Roman soldiers weren't acting mercifully. They were merely making sure he would stay alive to bear the full brunt of his sentence.

Jesus' way through the narrow streets of Jerusalem was probably a great spectacle. Luke tells us that large numbers of people followed him to Golgotha, that women were mourning and lamenting what was happening, and that two other criminals were led out with him to be executed.

The Romans had a twofold purpose in dragging condemned criminals through the streets in such a public display. They sought to increase the humiliation of the criminals themselves and of their families and friends. They also wished to remind the public of what might happen to them if they challenged Roman authority and power. This tactic, however, would have its full effect only if the criminals were kept alive to the very end. A criminal's premature death would fail to convey the desired effect in its entirety.

Jesus was kept alive to die a terrible death. His way to Golgotha represents a very refined form of cruelty, the kind designed to draw every last ounce of suffering and pain out of its prey before it's summarily put out of its misery.

As we meditate on this Mystery of the Rosary, we find ourselves identifying in some way with each character involved in its drama. We look inside ourselves and find that, like the Roman soldiers, we too have a great capacity for inflicting pain on others. We recognize times in our own lives when we have asserted our authority and power in ways that have overstepped the bounds of propriety. We see ourselves asserting our will over others and taking advantage of them for our own personal gain. We can even see ourselves not merely hurting someone else, but seeking to do so to the greatest extent possible. We may not kill them physically, but we do so in our minds by our failure to treat them with the dignity and respect they deserve.

Many of the other characters we encounter along the way of the cross also resonate in our hearts. Like the jeering crowd that followed Jesus through the streets of Jerusalem, we sometimes allow ourselves to be led by the volatile moods of those around us. Like the women who were mourning for Jesus as he made his way to his place of execution, we find ourselves at other times capable of great sensitivity and feeling for the suffering and pain of others. Like Simon of Cyrene, who helped Jesus carry his cross, we are sometimes pressed into the service of others at a moment's notice without a full appreciation of what we're being asked to do. Like the two criminals who walked with Jesus to Golgotha, we can become preoccupied with our immediate future and concerns of what will happen to us. At one time or another, each of these characters will resonate in our hearts—as will Jesus himself.

This Mystery of the Rosary invites us to travel with Jesus as he makes his final journey. We're not sure how long it took him to make his way to Golgotha. Measured in minutes and seconds, it could have been anywhere from a half hour to an hour, possibly more. When seen through God's eyes, however, Jesus' journey transcends time and has joined itself to eternity.

For us, that journey lasts an entire lifetime. As members of his Body, we're on a journey that closely adheres to the way of the cross. As his disciples, we're asked to renounce ourselves, take up our crosses daily, and follow him (see Matthew 16:24; Mark 8:34;

Luke 9:23). We do so by keeping our gaze fixed firmly on him, by uniting our suffering entirely with his, and by not counting the cost.

The way to Golgotha is a brutal and harrowing road to travel. Jesus, however, doesn't ask us to walk it alone. He goes not only ahead of us to show us the way—he is also beside us to encourage us with each difficult step and within our hearts to give us courage and strength to carry on. He walks with us each step of the journey. He falls when we fall and rises when we rise. Because we have united our suffering to his, he has united his to ours and promises to lead us through death and radically transform our lives.

The way to Golgotha leads to the empty tomb—and beyond. Even now, we are journeying there. In some respects we have already arrived. Jesus himself is leading the way.

Reflection Questions

- What crosses have you been asked to carry in your life?
- How heavy were they?
- Did you fall many times?
- Did anyone help you?
- Did you understand why you were carrying them?
- What effect did these crosses have on you?
- How did they shape your journey?
- Where did they take you?
- What did these crosses teach you about your relationship with Jesus?
- What did these crosses teach you about the walk of discipleship?
- Did you find meaning in your suffering?
- Were you able to look beyond it?

FIFTH SORROWFUL MYSTERY

THE CRUCIFIXION

When they came to the place called the Skull,
they crucified him and the criminals there,
one on his right, the other on his left.

LUKE 23:33

The Gospels tell us what happened (see Matthew 27; Mark 15; Luke 23; John 19).When Jesus reached Golgotha, he was nailed to the crossbeam and hoisted high in the air. His feet were nailed to a wooden support so that he would be able to breathe by pulling up from his arms and pushing down on his legs. If the legs were left dangling in the air, death would come much sooner. Above his head was placed an inscription listing the crime for which he was being executed. He hung on the cross for roughly three hours. Any strength he had left after the scourging, the crowning with thorns, and the journey to his place of execution flowed out of him through the open gashes in his hands and feet and through his struggle to breathe. Hanging from the cross, Jesus died a slow, painful death by asphyxiation.

Above his head was the inscription, "The King of the Jews." Below him, the soldiers cast lots for his clothing. The passersby jeered at him and mocked him. Most of his followers had abandoned him, although some of the women who had followed him from Galilee were watching from a distance. These included Mary Magdalene, Mary the mother of James and Joseph, and the mother of Zebedee's sons. At some point, some of these apparently moved closer to the cross; John's Gospel tells us that Mary his mother, the beloved disciple, and some of the other women were at the foot of the cross.

Darkness covered the land during the period Jesus hung on the cross, from the sixth hour until the ninth hour. At one point, one of the soldiers put a sponge soaked in vinegar on a reed and raised it to Jesus' lips. At around the ninth hour, Jesus cried out in a loud voice and breathed his last. Some accounts say that, at that moment, the curtain of the temple was split in two, as the earth quaked, boulders split, and many tombs were opened. Soon afterward, a soldier broke the legs of the two criminals beside Jesus. Seeing that Jesus was already dead, he pierced his side with a lance and, we are told, blood and water flowed out.

As evening approached, Jesus was taken down from the cross. Joseph of Arimathaea received permission from Pilate to bury Jesus. He took the body, wrapped it in a clean cloth, and laid it in a tomb that had recently been hewn out of rock. Some of the women noted its location.

The Gospels also preserve a number of Jesus' utterances from the cross which, down through the centuries, have become intimately connected to the meaning of the Christ event. His first words are a prayer of intercession, "Father, forgive them, they know not what they do" (Luke 23:34). Through these words, Jesus tells us that the only adequate responses to hatred and violence are quiet tears and a forgiving heart. Later, he turns to the good thief dying on a cross to his right and says, "Amen, I say to you, today you will be with me in Paradise" (Luke 23:43). Through these words, he teaches us it's never too late to open our hearts to God and seek forgiveness. Still later, he looks down to his mother and the beloved disciple and says, "Woman, behold, your son....Behold, your mother" (John 19:26–27). Through these words, he reminds us that our closest bonds are no longer those of blood, but those formed in faith and in the loving desire to do God's will.

At yet another point, Jesus cries out, "My God, my God, why have you forsaken me?" (Matthew 27:46). Through these words, he echoes the opening verse of Psalm 22, a hymn which moves from a cry of desperation to one of thanksgiving, trust, even praise. This is how Jesus demonstrates his complete and utter trust in the Father's plan for him.

Further on, his mouth parched and dry, he whispers faintly, "I thirst" (John 19:28). With these words, we recognize Jesus' thirst as closely tied to our own, simultaneously representing God's yearning for humanity and humanity's yearning for God.

As Jesus approaches death, he says, "It is finished" (John 19:30). These words of courage come from someone intent on carrying out the Father's will regardless of the consequences. Finally, as Jesus breathes his last, he cries out in a loud voice, "Father, into your hands I commend my spirit" (Luke 23:46). His final words from the cross are a prayer from the heart addressed to "Abba," his Father in heaven. Even as he dies on the cross, Jesus entrusts all that has happened to the Father's care.

Jesus underwent death for our sake. He died not for an idea or for an abstract concept, but for you and for me. He did so because of the Father's love for us, a love Jesus himself reflected in his entire being. Jesus truly was a man for others. He entered our world and became one of us. He gave himself to us to the point of dying for us. He became our source of nourishment and our cause for hope.

When meditating on this Mystery of the Rosary, we are called to ponder Jesus' death and see in it a manifestation of his love for humanity and a portent of his future glory. As we contemplate it, we will gradually see a reflection of our own dying to self and rising to new life.

As his followers, our lives and our deaths are intimately wound up in Jesus'. Because of his great love for us, his destiny has become our destiny. Jesus' life ends on the cross, but it is also radically transformed. The same is true for us. Our journey through life doesn't end in death. Jesus has died for us, but also risen for us. The tomb he was buried in could not contain the Father's love for him, nor will our tombs be able to withstand the power of the Father's love for us. Jesus has made sure of that. All we must do is look at him, trust him, and commend ourselves to his care.

Because of Jesus, we ourselves are but a few steps away from the empty tomb.

Reflection Questions

- Have you ever wondered what your death will be like?
- Can you picture it in your mind?
- Can you feel it?
- What reactions do you have to death?
- Are you afraid of it?
- Do you wish to escape it?
- Are you prepared for it?
- Are you ready to meet it?
- What would you want your last words to be?
- Would they express love and forgiveness like Jesus' last words?
- Does Jesus' death teach you anything about your own?
- How would you describe the relationship between the two?

PART IV

THE GLORIOUS MYSTERIES

The final five decades of the rosary celebrate the glories of Jesus and Mary, highlighting the wonderful fruits of our redemption and seeking to keep alive in us the hope that we will one day share in them fully.

The first decade, the *Resurrection*, peers into the empty tomb and sees through the eyes of faith the presence of the risen Lord. It asks us to look beyond the grave to the transformation we ourselves will one day undergo.

The second decade, the *Ascension*, ponders Jesus' glorious return to the Father. It reminds us of the rightful place of the Son of God and bids us to honor him with all the honor and praise his position deserves.

The third decade, the *Descent of the Holy Spirit*, celebrates the birth of the Church and the beginning of its first apostolic efforts. It reminds us of the communion of believers to which we belong and of the task we have been called to take up.

The fourth decade, the *Assumption*, tells us that Mary, by virtue of her being taken body and soul into heaven, already enjoys the fullness of redemption. It shows us our destiny, what we hope to share one day in all its fullness.

The fifth decade, the *Crowning of the Blessed Virgin Mary As Queen of Heaven*, celebrates Mary's queenship of heaven and earth. It reminds us of the special role she has played and continues to play in the mystery of our redemption.

Taken together, these Mysteries give witness to God's love for humanity and great power of that love. They tell us the glories of Jesus and Mary will one day be ours and, to a great extent, already are. They invite us to join them in the task of building the kingdom in this world and in the world to come.

FIRST GLORIOUS MYSTERY

THE RESURRECTION

They were utterly amazed. He said to them,
"Do not be amazed! You seek Jesus of Nazareth,
the crucified. He has been raised; he is not here."

MARK 16:6

The first Glorious Mystery is Jesus' Resurrection from the dead.

On the first day of the week, three days after his death and burial, some of Jesus' women followers found his tomb empty. The stone was rolled back, and his body was nowhere to be found. At first they thought his body had been carried away, but within a short while some of his disciples began saying they'd seen him.

Mark 16 says Jesus appeared first to Mary Magdalene, then to two disciples as they where on their way in the country, and finally to the Eleven at Galilee. Matthew 28 says that Jesus first appeared to two women, Mary Magdalene and Mary the mother of James, then to the eleven disciples at Galilee. Luke 24 preserves accounts of Jesus' appearances to the two disciples and then to the apostles. John 20 asserts that Jesus appeared first to Mary Magdalene and then to the disciples on three different occasions.

In 1 Corinthians 15, Saint Paul says Jesus appeared first to Cephas (Peter), then to the Twelve, then to more than 500 brothers at the same time, then to James, then to all the apostles, and finally to Paul. The tradition also developed early on that Jesus appeared first to his mother, Mary, his earliest and most faithful disciple.

His appearances are said to have taken place in both Jerusalem and Galilee. Something was different about him, for people didn't always recognize him right away. He appeared to individuals and to groups, often in the context of a meal. He was flesh and blood, but somehow gloriously transformed. According to John 20, he still bore the marks of his crucifixion on his body. These wounds remind us that new life comes to us only by first passing through death.

Although the accounts vary about the circumstances, number, and order of Jesus' appearances, all affirm that he overcame death and appeared to his inner circle of followers. It is from this tightly knit group that the Easter proclamation, "He is risen!" came to be. It is from them that the earliest Christian community was formed. It is from them that the Good News was preached and, through the movement of the Spirit in their lives, spread like wildfire.

The Church's proclamation of Jesus' resurrection rests upon the eyewitness accounts of these early disciples. Their experience of faith remains qualitatively different from our own, for they claimed to have seen Jesus living in a transformed and glorious state after his death.

Without the unprecedented boldness and resiliency of these claims, the Christian project would have nothing distinctive in its message and probably would never have gotten off the ground. Based on this testimony, we believe that the deepest yearnings of our hearts will one day be fully realized. We affirm that the transformation wrought by God in Christ will also be extended to us. We see a sharing in the life of the risen Lord as the ultimate destiny of all humanity, something that can be impeded only by a stubborn persistence in the life of sin.

Belief in the risen Christ keeps alive the hope that after death our own lives will not end, but merely change. Because of Christ's resurrection, we look forward to a transformed existence in the hereafter, one in continuity with our own lives on earth. Sustained by a prayerful response to the contemporary challenges of Christian discipleship, this hope forms the basis on which life in the resurrection is anticipated even in the present.

Through our participation in the ministry and life of the Church, we receive a foretaste of this transformed existence, especially when we partake of the sacraments around the table of the Lord. Jesus' disciples recognized him in the breaking of the bread at the Eucharist (see Luke 24:30). It is there where Christians, even to this day, gather to do the same.

Jesus' resurrection was an event both in and out of time. It is impossible to say what exactly happened or to know what an objective observer would have seen with the naked eye. The most telling evidence we have that something extraordinary did, in fact, occur is the transformation that took place in the lives of Jesus' followers. These people were simple, ordinary folk with their feet planted firmly on the ground. Whatever they experienced, they were thoroughly convinced that Jesus had risen from the dead and had appeared to them. Their lives were fundamentally changed by what they experienced, so much so that they were willing to die for it.

Because of their experience of the risen Lord, the fear of death no longer had a hold over them. Jesus' message of selfless love became the motivating and guiding force of their lives. It's meant to be the same for us.

As we meditate on this Mystery of the Rosary, let us ask the risen Lord to make the power of his love rise within our hearts and transform us. Let us ask him to help us die to ourselves so that we, like those who experienced him on the first Easter morning, might live totally for others. Let us ask him to transform us by the power of his love and to follow in his footsteps without ever counting the cost.

Reflection Questions

- What does Jesus' resurrection mean to you?
- Do you find it difficult to picture?
- Do you find it even harder to believe?
- How deeply do you believe in it?
- Do you assent to it intellectually?
- Is your heart in it?
- How does it affect your life?
- Does it add anything to the way you live?
- What does Jesus' resurrection tell you about yourself?
- Where does it point you?
- How does it direct you?
- What hope does it give you?
- Is that hope well founded?

SECOND GLORIOUS MYSTERY

THE ASCENSION

Then the Lord Jesus, after he spoke to them,
was taken up into heaven and took his seat
at the right hand of God.

MARK 16:19

The second Glorious Mystery is the Ascension of Jesus into heaven. Jesus appeared to his disciples several times after his resurrection and commissioned them to spread the Good News throughout the world, forgiving sins (see John 20:21–23) and baptizing in the name of the Father, Son, and Holy Spirit (see Matthew 28:19–20). At some point, however, it was time for Jesus to return to his rightful place at his Father's right hand in heaven.

Although they imply it, the Gospels of Matthew and John make no explicit mention of Jesus' return to the Father. Mark 16 mentions it at the very end, as a necessary prerequisite to the disciples to carry on their own ministry of healing and preaching. Luke's Gospel (24:50–53) and his follow-up volume, the Acts of the Apostles (1:6–11), provide more vivid details.

In these accounts, Jesus spends time with his disciples after his resurrection, opening their minds to understand all that was written about him in the Law and the Prophets. After forty days, he takes them to the outskirts of Bethany, lifts up his hands, and blesses them. He instructs them to wait in the holy city until they receive the Holy Spirit. Then they are to be his witnesses not only in Jerusalem, but throughout Judea and Samaria and to the ends of the earth. He then withdraws from them and is taken up to heaven in a cloud. As they stare into the sky, two men in white come to them and say, "Men of Galilee, why are you standing there looking at the sky? This Jesus who has been taken up from you into heaven will return in the same way as you have seen him going into heaven" (Acts 1:11).

Jesus' ascension represents an important facet of the mystery of the Christ event. It reminds us that Christ's redemptive action not only heals humanity, but also elevates it to new heights. Through Jesus' suffering, death, and resurrection, we are able to participate in Jesus' divine sonship. Because of this sharing, we have the hope of one day joining him at the right hand of the Father. Jesus' ascension is not simply a return to his rightful place with the Father as things were before his Incarnation. At his ascension he carries his transformed humanity with him into the presence of the Father.

With that humanity, he also carries humanity's deepest hopes. Jesus' redemptive action raises humanity to new heights, enabling it to be even better than before its tragic fall from grace. His ascension into heaven represents the priority of place that God's New Creation will have in the Father's plan.

Because of his divine sonship, Jesus—the New Man—now sits at the right hand of the Father. Through his passion, death, and resurrection, we can share in that sonship and join him as he enters the Father's presence. As the author of Ephesians so eloquently asserts, God the Father "destined us for adoption to himself through Jesus Christ, in accord with the favor of his will, for the praise of the glory of his grace that he granted us in the beloved" (Ephesians 1:5).

As members of his Body, we have a place with Jesus at the right hand of the Father. We will join him there, however, only when the reign of God enters the world in all its fullness. When asked when this would occur, Jesus tells his disciples that it's not for them to know times or dates that the Father has decided by his own authority (see Acts 1:7). Jesus says they will soon receive the Holy Spirit, who will empower them to be his witnesses throughout the world (Acts 1:8).

Jesus ascends to the Father so he can be present to his disciples in this new and powerful way. He leaves them so he can give them his Spirit to abide in their hearts continually. As a result, he will be able to give them his gifts, guide them in their apostolic mission, and carry out through the sacramental action of the Church the work of sanctification made possible by his death and resurrection.

When reflecting on Jesus' paschal mystery, the early Christian community came to see that it contained many intricate and closely related facets. The ascension is the aspect of this mystery that emphasizes completion of Christ's redemptive action and his return to the Father.

Jesus' ascension lays the groundwork for the coming of the Spirit and the Church's apostolic mission. It reminds us that our destiny is to join Christ at the right hand of the Father. It also makes clear to us that Jesus, while present to us through the Spirit, is mysteriously absent from our midst and will continue to be so until he comes again to fully restore his kingdom. This tension between Christ's presence in the Church through his Spirit and his absence from our midst because of his return to his Father, preserves the "already, but not yet" character of the kingdom's presence in the world both today and until the end of time.

When meditating on this Mystery of the Rosary, let us pray for the coming of the kingdom and ask the Lord to help us live our lives with the dignity and respect our adoptive sonship deserves.

Reflection Questions

- What does Jesus' return to the Father tell you about your own human destiny?
- Has he simply left you, or has he gone ahead to prepare a place for you?
- Do you look forward to what lies ahead?
- Are you moved by what God has done for you through Jesus Christ?
- Are you troubled by it? Disturbed by it?
- What does it mean to be an adopted son or daughter of the Father?
- What responsibilities come with such a privileged relationship?

THIRD GLORIOUS MYSTERY

THE DESCENT OF THE HOLY SPIRIT

And they were all filled with the holy Spirit
and began to speak in different tongues,
as the Spirit enabled them to proclaim.

ACTS 2:4

The third Glorious Mystery is the descent of the Holy Spirit upon the apostles.

At some point after his resurrection, Jesus met with his disciples and commissioned them to spread his message to the ends of the Earth. To assist them in their mission, he promised to send them a helper. John 20 describes this moment very vividly. Jesus comes to his disciples and says, "Peace be with you. As the Father has sent me, so I send you." He then breathes on them and says, "Receive the holy Spirit. Whose sins you forgive are forgiven them, and whose sins you retain are retained."

The Spirit is seen here as Jesus' breath. He gives his life force or principle of life to his disciples as a sign of his continuing presence. By the power of the Spirit, the disciples spread Jesus' message of love and forgiveness to the ends of the Earth. They proclaim the Good News of Jesus' resurrection from the dead and the dawn of the New Creation it inaugurates.

Pentecost is the birthday of the Church. Acts of the Apostles 2 describes in great detail the change that took place in the small remnant of Jesus' followers after they are clothed from on high with the power of the Spirit. Gathered in a single room, they suddenly hear something like a powerful wind from heaven. This noise fills the entire house and tongues of fire appear, separate, and rest on each of their heads. They are filled with the Holy Spirit and begin to speak in foreign tongues.

Those in Jerusalem at the time are amazed by the miraculous display of speech and wonder if this small group of Galileans has had too much wine. Peter speaks up and boldly proclaims that Jesus, whom they have crucified, has been raised up. He identifies Jesus as the long-awaited Messiah who has come to free them from their sins.

Some 3,000 people would come to believe that day. The community continues to grow as it devotes itself faithfully to the prayers, the apostles' instructions, the breaking of the bread, and the common life.

The pouring out of the Spirit at Pentecost enabled Christ to be present to his disciples in a new and powerful way. Through the Spirit, Christ is able to dwell in our hearts and enter into friendship with us. In doing so, he shares with each of us the bond of intimacy he shares with the Father. Another name for this bond is the *Spirit*.

The Holy Spirit is the soul of the Church. It vivifies the members of Christ's body and transforms them into a vital, living organism. Jesus acts in his Church through his Spirit. He does so primarily through the proclamation of his Word and the celebration of the sacraments.

Through the Spirit, Jesus heals our hearts and makes us whole. He also showers us with many gifts (see Isaiah 11:2–3). One of the most precious gifts he gives us is peace (see John 20:19–21). The Holy Spirit continually works for peace within our hearts, in our homes, in the workplace, in the community, in the Church, in the country, in the world. It does so by reassuring us of God's love for us and by gently encouraging us to follow in the footsteps of the Lord.

Mary, Jesus' mother, was a woman of the Spirit. She gave her loving *fiat* to God through the Spirit. She conceived and bore a son through the Spirit. She found the strength to withstand her many sorrows at the foot of the cross through the Spirit.

Mary was with the disciples on the day of Pentecost (Acts 1:14). The Spirit's descent probably came as no surprise to her. She was most likely a tranquil, calming presence in the middle of a great storm of excitement. Mary was full of the Spirit from the very first moment of her existence. She gave birth to Christ and to his Body, the Church. All of this was done by the power of the Spirit. Because of the Spirit, Mary is both Jesus' mother and our mother. She is gentle and loving with us. She has a compassionate and understanding heart. She is a bearer of peace who always leads us to her son.

Jesus promised that he would be with us always, until the end of the world (see Matthew 28:20). He does so primarily through the presence and power of his Spirit. The Spirit is always coming into our lives. It continues to enliven and vivify the members of Christ's body. It does so by interceding for us to God with inexpressible groanings deep in our hearts: "The one who searches hearts knows what is the intention of the Spirit, because it intercedes for the holy ones according to God's will" (Romans 8:27).

The Holy Spirit is God's presence within us. It has many titles: Paraclete, Helper, Divine Sanctifier, Advocate, Gift—to name but a few. It has so many names because of the great role it has played and continues to play in the history of salvation. Pentecost was only the first of many outpourings of the Spirit in the life of the Church.

When meditating upon this Mystery of the Rosary, let us thank God for the gift of the Spirit and the work it does in and through the Church. Let us ask the Lord to deepen our awareness of the

Spirit's presence in our lives. Let us ask for the grace to listen to its promptings and, like the disciples of old, respond to them boldly and without counting the cost.

Reflection Questions

- How has the Holy Spirit manifested itself to you? Through fiery tongues? In bold proclamation? Through inexpressible groanings? In the stillness of your heart?
- Are you able to sense the Spirit's presence in your life?
- Have you been receptive to its promptings, or have you stifled them?
- Where is the Spirit calling you?
- What gifts has it given you?
- Which of its many fruits are most manifest in your life?

FOURTH GLORIOUS MYSTERY

THE ASSUMPTION

I will put enmity between you and the woman,
and between your offspring and hers; He will strike
at your head, while you strike at his heel.

GENESIS 3:15

The fourth Glorious Mystery is the Assumption of Mary into heaven. Although there is scant Scriptural evidence for this belief, centuries of deep reflection by the Church on Mary's unique role in the mystery of redemption have made it a mainstay of Catholic doctrine. The Church's reflection came to a head on November 1, 1950, when Pope Pius XII solemnly defined this truth as a dogma of faith.

The dogma makes no claim about whether Mary died naturally or if she escaped death through a special grace from God. It does claim, however, that when her time on Earth came to an end, her body and soul were gloriously taken up into heaven. The intent of this dogma is to assert that, unlike other human beings who must wait until the end of time to experience the full fruits of Christ's redemption, Mary received them as soon as she completed her earthly sojourn. It is fitting that someone should currently experience the full fruits of the redemption won for us by Christ's paschal mystery. Mary's open and heartfelt *fiat* to God's plan for her makes her the most appropriate candidate. We look to her and see in her the fullness of what we ourselves long for and hope one day to fully enjoy.

Every doctrine of Mary ultimately tells us something about the mystery of Christ. The dogma of the assumption is no exception; it gives us deep insights into the extent and power of Christ's redemptive grace. That grace, it tells us, is not bound by the dimensions of space and time. It acts wherever and whenever it pleases in accordance with the wishes of divine providence.

Mary doesn't have to wait until the end of time to experience the full fruits of Christ's redemption. Because of her special role in God's redemptive plan, she was especially chosen to experience the fullness of those fruits beforehand. Mary's whole person has been wondrously transformed and is at this very moment replete with heavenly glory. Every aspect of her being—body, soul, and spirit—rests in the divine presence and enjoys the totality of God's redemptive love. She is the first to experience the fullness of redemption. As Saint Paul himself states: "Just as in Adam all die, so too in Christ shall all be brought to life, but each one in proper order" (1 Corinthians 15:22–23).

Mary is Jesus' mother and his first disciple. She followed him through life, from the moment of his birth to his terrible death on the cross. It's fitting that she be the first of us to follow him into heavenly glory.

As might be expected, the dogma of Mary's assumption also tells us something about ourselves. Mary is not a myth or symbol, but a real, historical figure. Her assumption into heaven reminds us of the fullness of life to which each of us has been called. What Mary enjoys in God's presence, we too hope one day to possess. She represents not an unattainable goal, but a concrete transformation that each of us longs for and hopes one day to enjoy.

Mary has gone before us and is preparing the way for us. Seeing her enjoying the fullness of heavenly glory, we are encouraged to continue our own earthly pilgrimage with eager expectation.

We too hope to share in the fullness of Christ's redemptive love. Although our time has not yet come, we see in Mary's assumption a concrete indication of its mounting approach: "With the Lord one day is like a thousand years and a thousand years like one day" (2 Peter 3:8). Mary's assumption tells us that at least one human being has already entered into the fullness of eternal life and that we can also fervently hope to one day make it there.

From beginning to end, Mary's life on Earth was somehow tied up in Christ's redemptive action. The dogma of her assumption tells us that the same is true for her life in heavenly glory. Because she has experienced the fullness of Christ's redemptive action, Mary has a special place in heaven and continues to draw others to her son through her powers of intercession. Mary, the mother of Christ, is also the mother of his Body, the Church. From her place in heaven, she looks out for the well-being of her children and does all she can to help them make their way to her son.

As we meditate on this Mystery of the Rosary, let us turn to Mary and bring to her our every need. Let us ask her to help us walk in holiness so we might join her at her son's side. Let us ask her to intercede for us so we might cooperate more fully with the graces God gives us. Let us ask her to watch over the rest of God's creation so that it might one day enter with us into the New Creation that her assumption into heavenly glory reveals.

Reflection Questions

- Does the dogma of Mary's assumption seem almost too good to be true?
- Does it trouble you in any way?
- If so, do you know why?
- Does it tell you anything about the mystery of Christ's redemptive love?
- What does it have to do with you?
- Does it capture your imagination?
- Does it tell you something about God's love for you?
- Does it promise you anything?
- Do you believe in that promise?
- Does it increase your hope of one day becoming fully redeemed yourself?

FIFTH GLORIOUS MYSTERY

THE CROWNING OF THE BLESSED VIRGIN MARY AS QUEEN OF HEAVEN

*A great sign appeared in the sky, a woman
clothed with the sun, with the moon under her feet,
and on her head a crown of twelve stars.*
REVELATION 12:1

The fifth Glorious Mystery is the Crowning of the Blessed Virgin Mary As Queen of Heaven. Mary's coronation represents a fitting completion of a life totally dedicated to God. Her response to the angel, "May it be done to me according to your word" (Luke 1:38), was an invitation to God to use her in whatever way necessary to further his plan of redemption. Her *fiat* involved not one, but many decisions in her life to open herself to the Lord's love. Her holy *yes* to God was given not just once, but throughout her entire life. From her place in heavenly glory, she continues to affirm the power of God's love for humanity and for all creation.

Mary's queenship in heaven embraces not only redeemed humanity, but also the new creation. She walks in fellowship with God in a garden remade according to the divine plan. From her vantage point in heaven, she intercedes for us and calls us to take a place at her side. Mary is our queen and our Mother. She is Queen of Peace and Mother of the Church. Her kingdom is the kingdom of her Son. It is not of the present world, but of the present world remade, where sin has been banished and where love, not hatred, motivates the minds and hearts of its inhabitants.

As queen of heaven, Mary actively seeks our spiritual and temporal well-being. She does so by the power of the Holy Spirit, who fills her soul with overwhelming joy, and by bringing our needs to the attention of her son. Jesus listens to his Mary as a loving Son. What he hears is guided by the deep bond of love the two of them have shared throughout their lives on Earth, especially now as they reign from heaven. Jesus and Mary walked this Earth together. They rule from heaven together, a place where love is the one and only binding rule.

As queen of heaven, Mary reminds us not only that we were created to dwell in God's presence, but also that God yearns to dwell in ours. Her very existence testifies to this truth. She is God's highly favored daughter who sits beside her son at the right hand of the Father and whose very soul is permeated by the presence of the Spirit. She is the queen of the New Jerusalem, the woman "clothed with the sun, with the moon under her feet, and on her head a crown of twelve stars" (Revelation 12:1). She is also queen of the human heart who, through the power of the Spirit, casts out the darkness within us and fills it with light of her son.

Mary gave birth to Christ in two ways: physically and in her heart. As queen of heaven she does all in her power to extend the reign of peace in our hearts through the power of prayer and intercession. Mary, our mother and queen, prays for us continually so that we, like her, will be able to say *yes* to God and *no* to the powers of darkness.

Membership in this kingdom requires our cooperation with divine grace. To enter it, we must humbly ask God to help us. As we do so, Mary actively joins in on our behalf and continues praying for us even after we have long grown weary. The help we receive through her intercession enables us to pick up our cross and follow in the footsteps of Jesus her son.

Mary meets us where we are and takes us a bit further along the way. With her help, we enter the kingdom as faithful disciples and members of the communion of saints. Mary stands at the center of this communion. She was her son's first and most faithful disciple. From heaven she works hard to expand its ranks and increase its influence over human hearts.

To have Mary as our queen means our deepest hopes are being realized. It tells us that the kingdom of God already reigns in her heart in the fullest way possible and helps us sense it taking root in our own. That kingdom is a place of gentleness and compassion, of mercy and forgiveness, of intimate friendship and deep, endearing love. Its dimensions go beyond those of space and time, for they defy concrete measurement and can be accessed only through the deep recesses of the heart. To find its gates, we must journey the hidden paths of the human heart and find our way.

Mary knows these paths well and has traveled them often with her son. Her heart is completely one with his. It reaches out to us and touches us. It offers us help in discerning the way we should walk. It offers to guide us—carry us, if need be—to the threshold of Jesus' heart. Once there, it invites us to enter, to rest, and to delight in his company.

A saint is a friend of God's, someone who communes with him and enjoys his fellowship. Mary is the friend of God *par excellence.* She is also *our* friend. It is wonderful to have a friend who is also a queen. Mary instructs us in the ways of the kingdom. She shows us the way to her son who, in turn, leads us in the way of peace.

As we meditate on this Mystery of the Rosary, let us thank the Lord for the gift of Mary, our mother and queen. Let us ask him to deepen our love for her, and let us ask her to deepen our love for him. Mary always leads us to Jesus. As queen of heaven, she rules wisely in the kingdom of her son. That kingdom is already in our midst and in our hearts. With Mary, let us pray for its fullness to reign in radiant beauty forever in our hearts.

Reflection Questions

- What does Mary's queenship tell you about the kingdom of God?
- What is the kingdom like?
- How do you imagine it?
- Do you long to travel there?
- Do you wish to enter it?
- Do you wish to be one of its citizens?
- What does it mean to pray for the coming of this kingdom?
- In what sense is it already here?
- In what sense is it yet to come?
- What does Mary's queenship tell you about humanity?
- What does it tell you about creation?
- Do you see in Mary and her son the first fruits of the New Creation?

PART V

CONCLUSION

The following words of Pope John Paul II offer a fitting conclusion to these meditations on the twenty-decade rosary:

> *The Rosary of the Virgin Mary, which gradually took form in the second millennium under the guidance of the Spirit of God, is a prayer loved by countless Saints and encouraged by the Magisterium. Simple yet profound, it still remains, at the dawn of this third millennium, a prayer of great significance, destined to bring forth a harvest of holiness. It blends easily into the spiritual journey of the Christian life, which, after two thousand years, has lost none of the freshness of its beginnings and feels drawn by the Spirit of God to "set out into the deep" (duc in altum!) in order once more to proclaim, and even cry out, before the world that Jesus Christ is Lord and Saviour, "the way, and the truth and the life" (Jn 14:6), "the goal of human history and the point on which the desires of history and civilization turn."*
>
> *ROSARIUM VIRGINIS MARIAE, 1*

May the meditations of this book inspire us as we continue to walk the path of discipleship. May they help us rediscover the usefulness of this venerable prayer form for contemplating the face of Christ by listening with Mary in the Spirit to the voice of the Father. May they heighten our awareness of the power of prayer, "the great means of salvation," for our lives and help us see in the Rosary of the Virgin Mary an easy and practical way to deepen our relationship with God.

Mary, Our Mother of Perpetual Help, pray for us.

ABOUT THE AUTHOR

Dennis J. Billy, a Redemptorist priest of the Baltimore Province, was professed in 1977 and ordained in 1980. He is professor, scholar-in-residence, and holder of the John Cardinal Krol Chair of Moral Theology at St. Charles Borromeo Seminary in Wynnewood, Pennsylvania. He holds a ThD in church history from Harvard Divinity School, an STD in spirituality from The Pontifical University of St. Thomas, and a DMin in spiritual direction from the Graduate Theological Foundation.

For more than twenty years, he was professor of the history of moral theology and Christian spirituality at the Alphonsian Academy of The Pontifical Lateran University in Rome. He has written or edited more than 25 books and has published numerous articles in a variety of scholarly and popular journals. Father Billy is also very active as a retreat director and spiritual director.